# An Introduction to
### Ultralight
# Gyroplanes


by
**Dave Organ**

First Published in the United Kingdom by

## Apex Publishing

Marshall House, Wymans Lane, Swindon Village, Cheltenham, Glos., GL51 9QF
Telephone 01242 233084; Fax. 01242 690034

January 2002

ISBN No. 0-954-1945-0-0

Printed and Bound by Stoate and Bishop (Printers) Ltd., Cheltenham, Glos. Tel. 01242 236741

# Acknowledgements

I would like to thank the following people and organisations, without whose help and contributions, this book could not have been written.

**The Civil Aviation Authority**

**Marshall Cavendish** — For allowing certain articles and sections of Aeronautical publications to be reprinted within these pages.

**Aeroplane Monthly** — For supplying many historical photographs.

**Popular Flying Association** — For their help in supplying current list of Gyroplane Instructors and Inspectors.

**Wing Commander K.H. Wallis, MBE, RAF Ret'd** — For his loyal support in supplying much of the material for the Chapter on the Wallis Series Gyroplanes and also for kindly acknowledging my efforts in his Foreword.

**Philip Jarrett** — For contributing many historical photographs and also for his published critical acclaim.

**Robin Morton** — For his enthusiastic support, written contribution and for supplying many photographs.

**John Kitchin** — For his critical appraisal of my original text and for his written contribution.

**Roger Savage**
**Marc Lhermette**
**Morag Jones**
**Mike Mee**
**Jason Hawkes**
**Ron Bartlett**
**Steve Fletcher from 'Today's Pilot"**
**Jim Montgomerie**
**Mike Goldring**
**Gerry Speich**
**Mel. Morris-Jones**
**Shirley Jennings**
**Colin Reeves** — For their unstinted help and support by supplying me with lots of photographs, images and other related information and for putting up with my constant phone calls, fax's etc. badgering them for more.

*Dave Organ*

# Contents

| CHAPTER | | PAGE No. |
|---|---|---|
| | ACKNOWLEDGEMENTS | 3 |
| | FOREWORD | 5 |
| | INTRODUCTION | 7 |
| 1 | ORIGINS OF ROTARY WINGED FLIGHT - THE PIONEERS | 9 |
| 2 | BIRTH OF THE AUTOGIRO - JUAN de la CIERVA | 14 |
| 3 | FROM PAST TO PRESENT | 20 |
| 4 | HOW IT WORKS | 26 |
| 5 | ACQUIRING YOUR OWN GYROPLANE | 29 |
| 6 | CAA REQUIREMENTS FOR TRAINING | 36 |
| 7 | GYROPLANE ALTERNATIVES AND OPTIONS | 44 |
| 8 | POWERPLANT OPTIONS | 45 |
| 9 | TWO SEAT TRAINING GYROPLANES | 48 |
| 10 | ROTOR THEORY AND HANDLING | 50 |
| 11 | SLEEPING PROJECTS | 54 |
| 12 | WHY DOES A GYROPLANE PORPOISE? | 57 |
| 13 | RADIOTELEPHONY | 59 |
| 14 | PROJECTS FROM ABROAD | 62 |
| 15 | PRE - ROTATORS | 65 |
| 16 | WALLIS SERIES GYROPLANES | 69 |
| 17 | TRAILERS | 71 |
| 18 | AIR COMMAND SERIES GYROPLANES | 76 |
| 19 | AIRWORTHINESS AND FLIGHT SAFETY | 78 |
| 20 | GYROPLANE INSPECTORS AND FLYING INSTRUCTORS | 80 |
| 21 | CONTACT ADDRESSES | 82 |
| 22 | GYROPLANE GLOSSARY | 87 |

# Foreword

by

## WG.CDR. K.H. WALLIS

### MBE, RAF RET'D

Amateur construction of aircraft is something of a "family vice", my father and uncle having completed their steel tube "Wallbro" Monoplane in 1910. My first venture was in 1936, with a "Flying Flea", but I had not made much progress before they were all grounded following a series of fatal accidents. This had an adverse effect on amateur construction for years.

Having learned to fly in 1937, I had the good fortune to get experience of very many types of aircraft, (but none with more than ten engines!). My flying and technical experience were useful in 1958, when I started to build an experimental light gyroplane. The very small scale appealed to me. I felt that it would owe me nothing if it would fly across the airfield at 18 inches above the ground!

It did that, and more, and I was soon being asked to demonstrate at military occasions and Air-Shows. As I became bolder, my previous flying experience sounded some warnings of potential hazards. From the lessons learned, but keeping the scale and principle, it was possible to design a thoroughly practical little gyroplane; one that would fly across the airfield, then the length of Britain, non-stop and with ease!

I can honestly say that the little gyroplane is the most enjoyable of all the aircraft I have flown; it really gives the feeling of flying. Able to fly safely in conditions that would cause problems with most other small aircraft it is thoroughly practical. Easily transported in ready-to-use condition on a road trailer, it can be stored and maintained at home. Furthermore, medical requirements to be met by gyroplane pilots, have now been brought into line with those for balloon and microlight pilots; a very sensible move that greatly eases the costs and complication of maintaining a licence.

The gyroplane's ability to fly very slowly, with no risk of a stall, make it potentially the safest of all aircraft. However, as with any aircraft, it needs to be properly designed, constructed and operated. Its apparent technical simplicity and forgiving nature can be abused, with potentially tragic consequences. A uniquely useful and enjoyable type of aircraft can unfairly acquire a bad reputation.

**"An Introduction to Ultralight Gyroplanes"** provides responsible advice for the amateur constructor/pilot on the whole subject, from the currently available plans and kits, training requirements and the many other matters leading to safe and enjoyable gyroplane flying. Take the advice, never think you "know it all", and you should have much happy flying in auto-rotation.

*RH Wallis*

# Introduction

My first booklet on Gyroplanes - **"A Guide to Gyroplanes in Britain"**, was published in 1991. It was originally conceived as a "one-off" publication, designed to help satisfy the need of those who had hitherto found information on this subject, difficult to find. The information contained within its pages was arranged in a simple and concise form in order to give the reader a step by step approach to the subject from its early beginnings through to the current scene and activities. This booklet became so popular over the intervening years that it has been updated and reprinted seven times.

In order to keep up with the ever changing scene, it has now become necessary to introduce a further updated edition. This book, although re-titled, still maintains the theme of its predecessors by concentrating on the scene here in Britain but also includes more detailed and up-to-date information with regard to current legislation, training, medicals, modifications etc., that hopefully, will keep the reader more fully informed. Although there are now several good books around on Gyroplanes, it has always been my intention to let this book serve as a first insight into what has become known as the **"Wonderful World of Gyroplanes",** and hope to convey to the potential Gyronaught that here in Britain, we do have a safe and well regulated approach to Gyroplane flying.

To all newcomers to this type of flying, my advice would be to read and absorb as much written matter as you can on this sport, talk to as many people connected with Gyroplanes as possible, organise a trial flight in a 2-seat Gyroplane or Gyro-Glider and then decide whether the thrill of flying one of these remarkable little aircraft is for you. This is how I now perceive the magic of flying Gyroplanes:

**Imagine** yourself sitting securely and held aloft on invisible wings with the vibrant sound of a powerful engine propelling you forward at a modest 50 to 60 m.p.h.

**Imagine** also, the wind on your face, the patchwork panorama of the countryside slipping beneath your feet and the exhilarating feeling of being in complete control. At the touch of the foot pedals or pressure on the control stick, you can manoeuvre at will in any direction, even up or down in complete safety.

**Imagine** that for less than the cost of an average family car, being able to build and keep this small craft in your own garage or workshop - carry out your own maintenance and, when the weather is right and the urge to fly beckons, go flying for your aerial 'fix'. Show off your pride and joy at local events - they always attract a crowd, or enjoy the comradeship of like-minded aviators at fly-ins or rallies - sharing each others experiences and aspirations.

This is only part of what's in store when you own and fly a Gyroplane, an aerial steed - a **"Pegasus"** that is so safe to fly, it cannot stall - even at zero airspeed. It can take off and land in the average farmer's field and should the engine stop, it can be landed safely under complete control. Even on breezy days this type of flying can be the envy of those who are constrained by the limitations of conventional aircraft.

If this "magic carpet" style of flying appeals to you, then by purchasing this book, you have begun the road to discovering the **"Wonderful World of Gyroplanes"**.

## Now That's Flying

Dave Organ

*Marc Lhermette Flying his immaculate RAF 2000 GTXSE over Leeds Castle in Kent*

# Chapter 1

# The Origins of Rotary Winged Flight
# The Pioneers

This first Chapter is intended to shed some light into the origins and progressive attempts made by the early pioneers at achieving flight with rotating wings. Man's fascination with this form of flight goes back many centuries and it is difficult to attribute its development and eventual success to any one individual. Certainly, a few names do spring to mind as being the main contenders - those who, in the early part of this Century eventually succeeded in transforming a dream into a reality. The earlier pioneers however, should not be dismissed lightly, as their contribution probably inspired those later and more successful individuals.

The earliest known form of rotating wings were probably the Chinese 'Flying Tops' used as toys around 400BC. They consisted of a short stick, spliced at one end into which were forced four feathers. Looking much like a four rotor assembly atop a rotor shaft,

the children would either spin the stick between the palms of the hand or by twisting cord around the stick and giving it a quick tug. The feathers, fixed with a slight angle of attack, acted like rotor blades and created a lifting force which sent the top soaring.

In the following centuries, after the decline of the ancient civilisations, there is no evidence of further development. In 1483, Italian Artist and Engineer, Leonardo Da Vinci conceived a screw or helix designed to screw up into the air. This was only one of his many ideas of man powered flight but was the first to suggest flight by means of a lifting airscrew. Made from

*Leonardo's Helix*

linen and coated with starch to seal the pores, it was suggested that rotation should be swift in order to rise high. It isn't known if he ever constructed such a machine and propulsion would certainly have been a problem. Models of Da Vinci's ideas and sketches are still on public display at his home - Clos Luce in Amboise on the River Loire, France.

The first power driven airscrew model was designed and flown by a Russian, Mikhail Lomonson, a notable Astronomer and Physicist who was to eventually earn the title "Father of Russian Science". His interest in aeronautics led to a design, powered by a clock spring which he demonstrated to the Russian Academy of Sciences in July 1754 he called his invention "Aerodynamic".

The earliest known European model helicopter that actually flew was created by two Frenchmen. In 1784 Monsieurs Launoy and Bienvenu combined their interests and talents and produced a spring driven, contra-rotating rotor system working on a single vertical shaft. The rotor blades were made of feathers and the fact that they contra rotated, effectively cancelled out any torque effect. This device was demonstrated at the French Academy of Sciences and flew unaided to quite a height.

Launoy and Bienvenu's model

In England one of the first and probably the most notable pioneer of manned flight was Sir George Cayley. Well known for his experiments with kites and fixed wing models, Sir George did hold a certain fascination with vertical flight and rotating wings. He was quick to emphasise the importance of being able to rise vertically, to hover and move forward and his drawings certainly showed a determination to tackle these problems head on. His design of 1842 consisted of two sets of contra rotating rotors or fans, two pusher propellers and two rudders. Each of the four rotors consisted of eight segments, each with the ability to turn at its root. This feature enabled each segment to increase its angle of attack for vertical take off and landing and to lie flat for level flight. Although lack of a suitable power source prevented such a machine from being built it did contain most of the ingredients now known to be essential for stable and efficient flight.

Another Englishman, Mr W.H. Phillips was probably the first to tackle the illusive propulsion problem. In 1842, he designed a steam driven, single rotor system that delivered steam up the central shaft, along the hollow rotors and out at their tips. This early form of jet propulsion was a novel alternative in its day and although it did manage to fly, the total weight of the machine prevented it from becoming a serious man-carrying aircraft.

On the steam theme, Frenchman Vicomte Ponton d'Amecourt patented a twin rotor, steam driven model in 1861 which flew in 1863 and is now in the French Air Museum. D'Amecourt teamed up with two like minded men Landelle and Nadar to form a small group of aviation enthusiasts intent on furthering research into rotary winged flight - later referred to as the "Triumvirat Hélicoïdal" - incidentally  D'Amecourt was responsible for creating the word helicopter, derived from the Greek Helicos (Helix) and Pteron (wing).

Others followed suit as steam became a popular power source and Italian, Enrico Forlanini designed a 7.71b engine which lifted his model 30 ft and hovered for around 30 seconds.

With the turn of the century, came the breakthrough in propulsion systems with the development of the relatively lightweight petrol engine. French designer Louis Breguet was first to successfully utilise this power source when, in 1907 his man carrying machine "Gyroplane No 1" lifted itself to a height of just 2ft, piloted by a Monsieur Volumard and held steady by four assistants. This was hailed by many as the first true vertical take off aircraft.

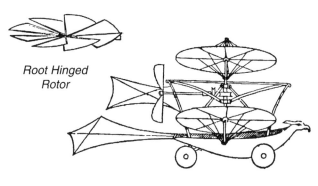

*Root Hinged Rotor*

*Sir George Cayley's Design*

Another Frenchman, Paul Cornu, improved on Bréguet's success and on November 7th 1907, his twin rotor machine, powered by a 24 HP Antoinette engine, lifted off without restraint to a height of 6ft and lasted about 20 seconds.

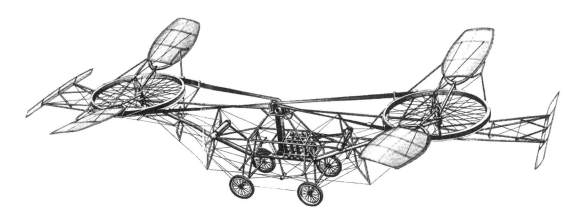

*Cornu, 1907*

A Danish engineer, Jacob C. Ellehammer started experimenting with aircraft designs in 1905, two years after designing and building probably the world's first 3 cylinder radial piston engine. His interest in rotary winged flight started in 1910 and in 1911, after carrying out several experiments, constructed a scale model helicopter. This, he transformed a year later into a full sized machine - the 36 hp air-cooled radial piston engine powering the rotors and a conventional tractor propeller.

The rotors consisted of two sets of contra-rotating rings mounted on a single shaft axis and each had six paddle vanes equally spaced around its circumference. Each paddle was mounted on a horizontal axis and could be made to change its pitch angle by an ingenious system of control wires leading back to the cockpit - the pilot therefore having

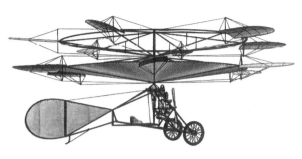

*Ellehammer 1912*

a small degree of control. The lower ring was covered in fabric for increased lift and both rotor systems were driven via a gearbox and hydraulic clutch - all designed by Ellehammer.

First tethered flights were carried out indoors and the first free vertical take-off flight was made in 1912. Later experimental flights came to an end in 1916 when the machine overturned on take-off and was wrecked.

Although power source problems had now been largely overcome, there still remained the problem of controlability. Vertical ascent was now possible but directional stability and forward movement still remained unsolved. In 1922, a Russian emigrant to the United States, Dr George De Bothezat, designed a helicopter for the US Air Corps. His machine, powered by a 180 HP Le Rhone engine, flew on 18th December 1922 and rose to a height of 6ft. Each fan-like rotor blade on this huge aircraft was another design that had the ability to change its pitch angle, much on the lines of Sir George Cayley's model, a century earlier. Later, this aircraft rose to over 30ft and lifted a total of 4400 lbs all-up weight before being finally abandoned as too complex and costly to continue.

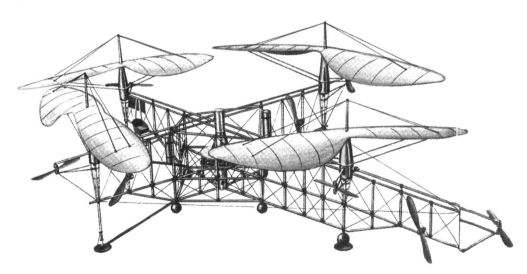

*Oemichen, No. 2 1924*

The lightweight, air cooled Le Rhone rotary engine now seemed to be the popular choice of most experimenters and Frenchman Etienne Oemichen, a Peugeot Motor Engineer used a 180 HP Le Rhone to power his new aircraft. This was an improvement on Bothezat's design and incorporated four, twin bladed rotors and eight propellers. Five were for stability, one for steering and two for forward flight. Although rather cumbersome with its array of whirling propellers, this machine set the first helicopter distance record of 1181ft. In May 1924, it flew 5500 ft at a height of 50 ft to win a cash prize from the French Air Ministry. Later it achieved the record payload lift of 200 KG up to 3ft.

In Spain, the Marquis Raul P. Pascara had been experimenting since 1919 and his third attempt at vertical flight was another significant step forward. His design was of a single shaft axis on which were mounted two sets of contra-rotating

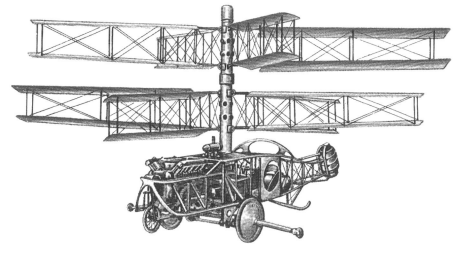

*Pescara, No3, 1924*

rotors. Each rotor had eight blades, each pair representing a biplane type brace and wire assembly and consequently had 16 lifting surfaces. The important point of this machine was that Pascara had included a mechanism for in-flight changes in rotor pitch and tilt. This degree of control enabled the machine to climb to 6ft and move horizontally 273ft. In January 1924, he had improved this by flying 1640ft, turned round and flew back again.

At around this time while Bothezat, Oemichen and Pascara were busy perfecting their multi rotor systems, another young Spaniard was pursuing the same objective but from a completely different approach.

**Juan De La Cierva,** an Engineer and Mathematician, was progressively developing a single rotor machine that utilised the elements rather than a mechanical device to achieve the desired lift. In an age when the new lightweight power plants were considered as essential for this purpose, Cierva's early attempts were often treated with ridicule. Undaunted however, he persevered and the eventual success of his work was to completely "revolutionise" rotary wing development and ultimately led to the birth of the helicopter.

**Chapter 2**

# Birth of the Autogiro
## Juan de la Cierva

Cierva's story has been told many times - all with varying degrees of accuracy. In order to appreciate the value of his contribution to aviation, it is important that it is retold here as a constructive sequence of events without the clutter of too much technical detail.

Born in 1895 as Juan de la Cierva Y Cordonia (Cordonia being his mother's name), Juan first had an interest in aeronautics when he was 14 years old. In 1911, he constructed, with the help of two friends, several model aircraft and two gliders. They then bought the remains of a wrecked biplane and rebuilt it so successfully that it became the first Spanish aircraft to fly. Its vivid red colour scheme became a familiar sight in the Madrid area but it finally fell to pieces through old age.

Before graduating from the Madrid Civil Engineering School in 1918, Cierva had competed for a 10,000 dollar prize, offered by the Spanish Government for the design and construction of a large bomber aircraft. His contribution was a biplane of 80ft wingspan, powered by three Hispano Suiza engines and which incorporated several advanced ideas for its day. While on its maiden flight in 1919, this excellent aircraft was destroyed while attempting a turn at too low an airspeed while too near the ground. Although the result was a mass of tangled wreckage, the pilot - a Captain Rios, escaped with a few minors cuts and bruises. Commenting on this event, Cierva later stated that "the pilot had misjudged his minimum flying speed while too close to the ground. Had the same thing happened while he was flying high, he could probably have recovered control and brought the aircraft safely down".

This event, although of little significance then but which could so easily have ended a promising career, was the trigger that set Cierva off in search of a "stall proof" aircraft that

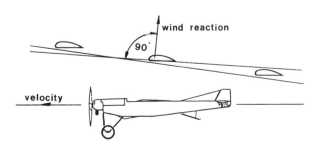

could take off, fly and land safely at very low airspeeds. To achieve this, Cierva had decided that the lifting surfaces i.e. the wings, had to move faster through the air than the aircraft itself but also relative to it. His first conception of this idea was of an aircraft somehow having a constantly forward sliding wing, fixed above the fuselage with its linear path inclined rearwards from the direction of flight. He had calculated that by giving the wing a degree of freedom to slide easily, the resultant wind reaction from the forward moving aircraft, would cause the wing to move forwards with a greater velocity than the aircraft itself. The difficulty lay in transposing this idea into a practical closed circuit mechanism and several variations of rotational systems were considered. Most were eventually thought to be too complicated to develop mechanically so the idea of a rotational system supported on a pylon above the aircraft, seemed a more practical method.

In 1920, Cierva started experimenting with actual aircraft of World War I vintage. He soon discovered that his theories proved correct and that the lifting surfaces (the rotors) would rotate freely, and effectively move forward at a faster rate than that of the aircraft, but there was a problem concerning stability. Because the forward moving blade created more lift than the retreating one, his aircraft tended to capsize.

To counteract this phenomenon, Cierva decided to mount a second set of rotors on the same axis but designed to rotate in the opposite direction. This, he thought would equal out the lift imbalance and solve his problem. However, the practical tests proved disappointing, largely it was thought, due to the airflow conditions through both sets of rotors. Further tests were carried out using rubber-band powered models and one of these flew

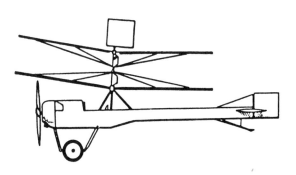

*Cierva C.I. Single Aileron, Contra-Rotating Co-Axial Rotors*

exceptionally well. Its rotors were made of a very flexible material known as rattan and Cierva realised that it was this flexibility, which allowed the advancing blade to rise and the retreating one to fall, that balanced out the unequal lifting forces. This trial and error method had, at a stroke, created the breakthrough he was looking for and soon he had designed and installed a small hinge at the root of each blade that allowed a small up and down flapping movement as various lifting forces were applied.

On January 9th 1923, Cierva's fourth machine, a converted Hanriot Scout, powered by a Le Rhone rotary engine, took off under complete control from Getafe Airfield near Madrid. Piloted by Army Lt. Alejandro Gomez Spencer, this flight, although short, was a great step forward for rotary winged flight. The concept of autorotative wings had been proved and it set the standard for future development, not only for the Cierva machines but also for helicopters as well. The idea of the flapping hinge, was, unbeknown to Cierva, used by Frenchman Charles Renard on his experimental machine back in 1904 but Cierva's use of it in a successful aircraft was a notable first.

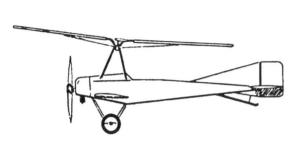

*Cierva C.4 Flapping hinges, ailerons on spars. First successful Autogiro.*

The media of the day referred to Cierva's aircraft as the windmill plane but he made short shrift of that idea, emphasising the fact that the blades of a windmill are blown around whereas his machine's blades are flown around into the oncoming airflow. Other more descriptive names emerged - "The Spanish Windmill", the "Corkscrew Plane" and even an "Autogyroscope". Cierva's own baptism for his invention was "Autogiro" which was eventually adopted as the generic term given to this type of aircraft i.e. Autogyro, Gyro or Gyroplane.

Still improving his designs, Cierva brought his C6A model to Britain in 1925 and on 20th October, demonstrated it at Farnborough for the Air Ministry. The C6 was based on the fuselage, engine and tail unit of a British Avro 504K and although there were a few problems, particularly with regard to rotor pre-spinning due to the lack of wind, the Ministry were nevertheless impressed enough to order one machine. This was built by AVRO in 1926 - the same year that Cierva, with the help of industrialist James Weir, set up the Cierva Autogiro Company Ltd.

Further demonstrations of modified C6's were carried out in France and Germany during 1926 but in February 1927 there was a slight hiccup when a near fatal accident was caused by a blade detachment. The reason was determined as blade root fatigue due to periodic bending, and the remedy was to install another hinge called a "drag hinge". This allowed each blade to move slightly in its fore and aft plane of rotation to 'hunt' its natural position and was another step towards the development of the fully articulating rotor head.

In 1928, as part of a grand European tour, Cierva himself piloted the first Autogiro to cross the English Channel. The machine was a two seat C8L MkII registered No G-EBYY that took off from Croydon on 18th September and landed at Le Bourges. Later he flew on to Brussels. In all, over 3000 miles were flown and was hailed as a great

*Cierva C.8L Mk II G-EBYY*

success. The aircraft still exists today and is on display at the Musée De l'Air in Paris.

Another development was that of what today we call a pre-rotator - a mechanical arrangement that helps speed up the rotors before take-off, so shortening the take off run. A neat idea incorporated on a C19 MkIII was a tilting tailplane which deflected the prop wash upwards through the rotors so causing them to rotate. This worked quite well at the time but was eventually succeeded on later models by a mechanical drive shaft, clutched between engine and rotor head. This was a more effective device which of course was to lead directly towards a powered rotor system.

During the next few years, the news of a new rotor plane spread quickly and aircraft manufacturers throughout the world clamoured for their bite of the cherry. Licences were granted to build Cierva based machines in both Europe and the USA. In England, AVRO had been in production since 1926 and they were joined by De Haviland, Westland and Weir; in France, The Loire Co; in Germany by Focke-Wulf; in Russia by Kamov. In the United States where the first autogiro demonstrations took place in August 1929, Pitcairn and Kellett were the principal manufacturers later to be joined by the Buhl Aircraft Co. In April 1931, a Pitcairn Autogiro caused a stir when it landed and took off on the White House lawn in front of President Hoover, and Amelia Earhart set an autogiro altitude record of 18,400ft - things were moving fast.

Back with Cierva for the moment; further modifications on a C-19 in 1932 finally produced the "direct control" rotor head. With the use of an overhead joystick, the pilot was now able to control the aircraft by moving the rotor head like a universal joint, consequently eliminating the need for Ailerons. Slow speed flight, where airflow over the wing surfaces had little or no effect was also dramatically improved so the stub wings and Ailerons were dispensed with henceforth.

The advent of the Cierva C30 in April 1933 marked a new era in the development of rotary winged flight. Publicly demonstrated by Cierva on 27th April, the prototype G-ACFI was the first wingless autogiro to incorporate the direct control articulating head and a mechanical drive shaft pre-rotator. Over 100 C30's were built in England alone and it became the basic training aircraft at Cierva's flying school where, in 1938, 298 students qualified as Autogiro Pilots. Other manufacturers based their new designs on the C30 and as refinements were added, so manoeuvrability and precision flying improved. The Army, Police and Post Office operated C30s for various purposes and they were operational

The prototype Cierva C30, G-ACFI, first "direct control" autogiro. RAF versions named AVRO Rota

from ships, roof tops and city centres. Cierva still strived for perfection and sought an answer to the one limitation - that of take-off run in still air. Westland had been experimenting with direct take off on a C29 but were unsuccessful and Cierva wasn't keen on producing more C30 types until he had solved the problem. After experimenting with various types of inclined drag hinges that permitted each blade to vary its angle of attack according to the amount of torque applied, a modified C30 using a 2 bladed rotor, was publicly demonstrated at Hounslow Heath in July 1936 - the jump take off capability had arrived - but still needed refining.

Although ground resonance had been eliminated by using a two bladed rotor it still had an inherent vibration which Cierva was unhappy about. His ultimate dream was to develop what he called an "auto-dynamic rotor" which not only incorporated jump take-off, but also several other innovations. Eventually he developed a three bladed rotor system that was relatively free from ground resonance and without the two bladed vibrations. This system was used successfully on the C40 Autogiro which immediately went into production - The Royal Air Force buying a batch of five naming them Rota II.

Operation of the C40 was relatively simple. For take off, the blades were accelerated in fine pitch by the engine which was declutched when the desired rpm were attained. The loss of torque on the blades would cause them to swing forward on the angled drag hinges into positive pitch. The increase in lift causing the aircraft to leap into the air. The pilot would then gain forward speed in order to continue the autorotation of the rotor. In this manner the autogiro briefly became a helicopter, relying on rotor inertia to become airborne.

The RAF eventually acquired all production models of the C40 which were fitted with 180 hp Salmson engines and could accommodate two persons in a partially enclosed cabin. This design served as the culmination of Cierva's life's work and could almost achieve the vertical take-off capability of the now evolving helicopter.

*The Cierva C40 or Rota II L7589 -*
*"Jump" Take Off Autogiro*

Aviation suffered a very great loss indeed when Cierva lost his life in a KLM DC-2 airliner crash on 9th December 1936, while taking off in fog from Croydon Airport. This sad event prevented Cierva from witnessing the success of the C40 but his life's work on rotary winged flight led directly to the success of the helicopter.

# Chapter 3

# From Past to Present

With Cierva's death, rotary wing development changed course slightly and other designers came to prominence. One, who already had a financial interest in the Cierva Company was G & J Weir Ltd. of Cathcart, Glasgow. In 1932 they embarked on a programme of Autogiro design, the first of which was the W.1., also given the Cierva type designation C28. It was the result of a design team that included Dr J.A.J. Bennett and C.G. Pullin and featured a 28ft. diameter, two bladed rotor, powered by a 40 h.p. Douglas Dryad two cylinder air cooled engine. In May 1933, Cierva himself piloted its maiden flight and Alan Marsh followed with the remaining flight trials.

W.2 followed shortly afterwards with a more powerful engine, the Weir Dryad II of 50 h.p. and a modified rotor system for improved lateral control. Tailplane and fin were closer to the Cierva C30 model but subsequently changed for an improved version some time later. This particular model has survived to this day and is now resident in the Museum of Flight, East Fortune Airfield, North Berwick in East Lothian, Scotland.

*The Weir W2 single seat light Autogiro with modified tailplane*

W.3 was a much improved version, fitted with the Cierva "Autodynamic" rotor head for "jump" take-offs. Powered by a Weir Pixie I, four cylinder air cooled engine with improved landing gear and triple tail unit, this model first flew on 9th July 1936. It was later demonstrated at Hounslow Heath and Brooklands August Bank Holiday Motor Race Meeting.

W.4 was the last in the series and first flew at Dalrymple, Ayrshire on 6th January 1938. The engine was an uprated Weir Pixie as used in the W3 and incorporated several refinements such as a faired pylon, improved landing gear and a more robust transmission unit.

Although the Weir company's interest then turned to producing helicopters, they had gone a long way to prove the concept of a two bladed rotor system, making improvements and refinements with each successive model.

However, Weir's were not the only ones working in this field and due consideration should be given here to another rotary wing pioneer - **Raoul Hafner.**

Hafner was of Austrian descent and had already built two helicopters before coming to England in 1932. He brought with him his second machine, his RII, to be used as an experimental test bed. After learning to fly a C19 and a C30, Hafner's first British Autogiro was the A.R.III, built by Martin-Baker Aircraft Ltd at Denham. Designated G-ADMV, it first flew in September 1935 albeit with a three bladed rotor system - the head being of his own unique design. This machine had a chequered history following an accident at Farnborough and was struck off the register in April 1942.

At the outbreak of war in 1939, Hafner was interned as an "Enemy Alien" but then released when his talents were recognised by the Military. In 1940 he started designing a small man carrying machine which could enable an armed man to land where he wished rather than where his parachute might take him. His first attempt was a two-bladed rotor system which could be strapped to a man's back, the idea being that the rotors would fold back inside the aircraft but unfold and autorotate when the man jumped out. Sensibly this was only attempted with models, two of which did in fact work but the tests were soon dropped.

Hafner realised that although the concept was sound, a rotor system needed a secure anchor so a full size tubular framework was built which incorporated a tail fin for stability. The man/soldier could now sit partially inside, armed with a Bren gun and could tilt the central pivoted rotors with a small overhead control stick. This design was later developed as a rotary winged glider and tests at Ringway Airfield eventually led to the Mk I "Rotachute" making its first flight in February 1942. This, unfortunately overturned on landing and so did two further

*A MK III Hafner Rotachute*

flights. To correct the problem, the MK II machine was fitted with two main wheels instead of skids and further flight tests proved satisfactory.

The MK III version incorporated a larger tail fairing with a small tailplane and this became the first truly successful design which achieved a tow speed of 93 mph at up to 400ft in height - a later MK IV had a modified tailplane which incorporated outer vertical fins and over 20 machines were eventually produced.

Success with the "Rotachute", although never used in combat, led Hafner to design another two-bladed rotor system, this time on a 4 seater jeep. This became known as the "Rotabuggy" and although several successful tows were achieved, it was eventually dropped as a practical means of transporting military hardware. In 1944, Raoul Hafner's AR III construction company was bought up by the Bristol Aeroplane Company and Hafner became the Chief Designer of its new helicopter division, going on to design the Bristol type 171 Sycamore and the Type 173 10 seater, twin rotor machine which evolved into the Type 192 Bristol Belvedere.

Although Hafner's "Rotachutes" became virtual museum pieces in England, several found their way into the United States of America, where, a certain aeronautical engineer, **Igor B. Bensen,** managed to acquire one. In 1953, Igor Bensen set up his own aircraft corporation to investigate and carry out feasibility studies on small rotorcraft and Hafner's "Rotachute" was the basis of his first experiments. He flew the "Rotachute" as a Gyro-glider, later converting it into what became the B.I. mid jet which used a teetering rotor system with jet pods at the rotor tips. In all, Bensen personally test-flew over sixteen experimental rotorcraft out of which emerged the B-7 Gyro-Glider followed by his most successful powered rotorcraft, the B-8M. Powered by a McCulloch, 4 cylinder air cooled drone engine, the B-8M, with its numerous "add on" optional extras was the basis from which most of today's gyroplanes have evolved. It used a unique, two bladed

*Benson's B-8M Gyrocopter with overhead joystick and motorised pre-rotator*

teetering rotor system that balanced out the unequal lift of the opposing sides of the rotor disc. These machines sold worldwide in both kit and plans-built form and constructors were able to keep costs down by purchasing locally available materials and working on their machines as their time and budget would permit.

Here in Britain during the 1960's - several aviation pioneers started experimenting and improving on Bensen's design - most notable being Wing Commander Ken Wallis who went on to develop a whole new range of autogyros, each designed for a particular purpose and including many revolutionary features (See Page 69). Other popular types that were available commercially are still around today - these include the Campbell Cricket, Brooklands Hornet and Mosquito, McCandless and Ekin's Airbuggy - all powered by modified Volkswagen Air-cooled engines.

*A striking pose for the latest **Montgomerie - Merlin GTS** - this is Jim Montgomerie's latest model and at first glance it looks very similar to the original Merlin but the changes are quite radical. In line with recent research data, the propeller thrust line has been lowered to pass through the machine's centre of gravity. The propeller/keel clearance is maintained by introducing a stepped joint in the keel tube and main wheel suspension is achieved with the introduction of fully sprung and dampened struts.*
*Engine; Rotax 582 driving a 60" dia. Ivoprop adjustable pitch propeller. Cruise speed is 75 mph, with a rate-of-climb of over 900ft/min. Rotors are 23ft Dragon Wings.*

Today, development of Gyroplanes, as they are now more familiarly known, is at a much faster pace; modern technology, coupled with new materials and lighter, more efficient powerplants have all helped to accelerate interest and create public demand for a safe, simple and inexpensive form of recreational flying machine. Gyroplanes are mechanically simple in construction and stable in the air - hence their growing popularity. They are far more versatile than any fixed wing aircraft, are impossible to stall and yet are capable of speeds in excess of 100 mph. They can (in certain wind conditions), hover or even fly backwards, can descend vertically under complete control and can make safe, controlled landings, in the event of engine failure.

One positive step in Britain has been the introduction by the Aviation Governing Body - The Civil Aviation Authority (CAA), of a design code for gyroplanes - otherwise known as BCAR Section T and this now forms the basis from which new British designs have to comply. New machines are frequently in the pipeline but it can take at least five years for a new design to become **"type approved"**.

Other types are gradually filtering into this country from abroad but the Civil Aviation Authority (CAA) only allow their approval on what is known as the **service experience** method, i.e. - account is taken of their airworthiness data and track record supplied from the country of origin.

## *Fly Gyro!*

### magazine

Instructions:
To be taken once
every 2 months.

*Guaranteed*
to cure depression,
boredom, apathy and
many other conditions
which can afflict the
enthusiast of the
autogyro.

Not to be taken by mouth

***Fly Gyro!*** is a 'proper' magazine highlighting interesting gyro developments ***worldwide*** - past, present and future. The latest interesting ideas, experiments and gyro designs, gyro events in the UK and all over the world with reports and photos. Interviews with interesting and famous gyro personalities and designers, articles, 'Useful Tips & Tricks', and all edited by one of the UK's most active gyro flyers!

**£20** per year. Is it worth it? - ask anyone who takes it!!

To subscribe or for more information contact Mel Morris Jones.
Tel: 01398 323903. Fax: 01398 323185 e-mail mel@flygyro.com Alternatively, visit the website at **http://www.flygyro.com** where you can also subscribe online through our Secure Server. (By clicking on the links to any back issue - on our payment page - you can see 'miniature' versions of every single page of any back issue). Try just one copy if you like.

# Chapter 4

# How it Works

## Autorotation

Nature has applied the principle of autorotation for millions of years, seen in the whirling flight of the sycamore seed as it falls to the ground. Autorotation slows its descent and the wind has greater opportunity to disperse the seeds over a wider area.

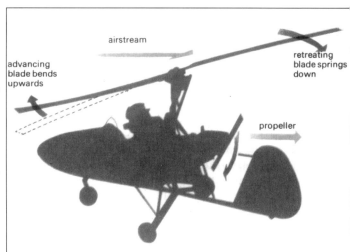

The windmill was probably the first human invention which used autorotation, by harnessing the wind to produce rotary motion. The idea of a flying windmill, where rotating sails produced a

*This picture shows how the advancing blade which creates more lift as it moves into the airstream, bends upwards to "store" energy which it releases by pivoting downwards as it retreats. This teetering of the rotor system balances the lift on opposing sides of the rotor disc; without it, the machine would roll over as it moved forward.*

wind to lift the machine, had a certain fascination with inventors, and among Leonardo da Vinci's thousands of drawings is an idea for flight along these lines. The real possibility for achieving such a machine was, however, delayed until development of the aerofoil and the aeroplane which embodied this device.

A windmill is basically an airscrew or propeller working in reverse, such that the air flowing over the sails is deflected by them, and exerts a force on the sails pushing them round. The sails effectively 'give way' to the wind and are pushed round by it.

As early as the Middle Ages, however, it was realized that if the sails were set at a very flat angle to the wind they would be made to rotate against the airflow and thus be 'pulled' round into the wind. The principle here is the same as with a sailing ship which can 'tack' close to the wind, meaning it can move forward against the wind, at a shallow angle to it, if the sails are properly set. In much the same way a glider moves forward as it descends through the air.

The rotor blades of an autogyro are shaped to achieve the same effect, and set at a shallow angle of about two degrees to the horizontal plane in which they rotate. The shape is that of an aerofoil which enables the blades to turn into the airflow rather than be pushed round by it.

When turning fast these rotor blades offer considerable resistance to the upward airflow, and it is their resistance that can be used to provide lift. The amount of lift created depends upon a compromise between the airspeed of the rotors, and the resistance the rotating blades offer to the airflow past them. In practice the desired lifting force is only produced when the blade speed greatly exceeds the forward speed of the machine.

# Take off

To take off, the rotor must produce adequate lift and it is necessary therefore to bring the rotor up to the required speed. This can be done in two ways.

The first and simplest way is to propel the machine forward and, by tilting the rotor system back, making use of the airflow through the blades to build up the rotor speed. This however requires a suitably long runway.

A second method involves more complex machinery but makes possible very short take-off distances. Here the rotor is brought up to speed by a linkage to the engine used to provide the forward motion. When the rotor has the correct speed, the linkage is disengaged. The machine is then allowed to move forward and take-off is achieved by tilting back the rotor system.

Some autogyros can 'jump-start' by over-speeding the rotor, using the engine. The drive is then disengaged, and the rotor pitch increased. The aircraft jumps, using the stored energy, and continues then in autorotation.

# Landing

When the engine and propeller speed are reduced, the forward speed will decrease and the autogyro goes into a steady descent path. The autorotation principle still applies, as the air flowing up and through the rotor maintains the rotor speed. A lifting force is therefore produced which, although

*A good example of an open framed **Benson B-8V**, powered by an 1834cc Volkswagen air cooled engine turning a 52" 2 bladed wooden propeller. This particular aircraft also includes a custom made instrument pod, extra long range fuel tank and a modified Campbell Cricket style tail unit.*

insufficient to maintain the machine's altitude, prevents it from falling like a stone. Even when the propeller is stopped, the autogyro will descend safely, under full control, from any altitude.

In this respect the autogyro is at some advantage over the helicopter since in the case of helicopter engine failure, the 'climbing pitch' angle of the rotors (about 11 degrees) would quickly stop them, with disastrous results. To keep his rotors turning the pilot would have to quickly reduce the pitch angle of his blades to that which provide 'autorotation' for a safe forced landing, but some valuable height may be lost in the process.

# Chapter 5

# Acquiring Your Own Gyroplane

Before committing yourself to purchasing a gyroplane, it would be very advisable to experience gyroflight first hand. This can be done either by arranging a test flight in one of the current 2 seat gyroplanes now flying in this country or have some tuition on a Gyro-glider. The latter is an unpowered 2 seat, side by side gyroplane that can be towed along a runway by a vehicle, attached to a suitable length of tow line. Manoeuvrability in the air can be somewhat limited due to the lack of propeller thrust over the tail surfaces but with no engine noise, and an instructor sat alongside, this type of machine is ideal for gaining initial handling experience and rotor technique, so necessary when training on your own machine. If, after either of these experiences, you decide not to proceed then you haven't broken the bank in order to find out.

However, assuming that you are bitten by the gyro bug, there are several routes into gyroplanes:

1.  Build a machine from plans, mainly
    Bensen or KB2                        Cost  £6,000-£8,000
2.  Build a machine from a kit
    (all parts supplied)                 Cost £8,000-£9,000
3.  Build a machine from pre drilled
    parts ready to assemble              Cost £8,000-£10,000 (2 seat machines
                                         from £18,000)
4.  Buy a new machine ready to fly       Cost £9,000-£12,000
5.  Buy a second-hand machine with
    a current "Permit to Fly"            Cost £3,500-£7,500
6.  Buy a partly built machine and continue
    construction. Cost varies depending on
    state of build but could be from around £1,500+

These last two options should be considered very carefully and you are advised to consult or take with you an experienced gyroplane constructor or inspector when you view the machine in question.

Most people opt to build their own Gyros from plans or an approved kit and this method, although sometimes tedious, does help to spread the financial load.

Help and advice is always available from within the British Rotorcraft Association and the Popular Flying Association and Approved Gyroplane Inspectors are usually on hand to offer the benefit of their experience and can sign out your machine during the stages of construction. If you have not already done so, join the PFA and BRA before starting your project.

*Gyro line-up at a Local Club Rally*

## Gyroplane Types

Gyroplane types now available include the ever popular Bensen B8V and B8R (V = Volkswagen, R = Rotax); Campbell Cricket (Mkl - Mk6), powered either by Volkswagen or Rotax; Brock KB2 - Rotax; Montgomerie-Merlins - Rotax; W.H.E. Airbuggy - Volkswagen; Everett - originally Volkswagen but later changed to Rotax; and a few remaining Brooklands Hornets and Mosquitoes - both Volkswagen powered.

Two seat machines include the open framed Montgomerie/Parsons tandem seating arrangement, powered by a Rotax 582 or more recently by a Rotax 618; the Italian VPM M16 tandem, powered by an Arrow 1000cc four cylinder 2-stroke (some are now being converted to Rotax 912 and Subaru - both being four cylinder 4-stroke engines); and the Canadian RAF 2000 fully enclosed, two seat, side by side, powered by a Subaru 2200 Legacy engine.

## Maintenance and permit renewal

In order to keep your Gyroplane in good and safe flying condition, you will need to have a copy of **The Owners Handbook for Ultralight Gyroplanes**. This book is a "must" for all Gyroplane owners and is available at a modest cost, through the PFA office at Shoreham. Gyroplanes operate on a "self maintenance" basis so you will either have to be capable of doing these tasks yourself or have a qualified engineer do it for you. Your local PFA Inspector will always be available with advice should you have a problem and when your annual **Permit to Fly** comes up for renewal, he will need to see written details of all the work carried out on your machine during the past 12 months. He will then inspect your Gyroplane and, if he is satisfied with the results, stamp and sign your maintenance log books. Your Gyroplane Inspector also supplies you with the appropriate

**Permit to Fly Application Form.** Filling it in is no great problem so long as you have all the facts relating to your Gyroplane's history and specification. After you've completed your part, call in your Inspector and when he is satisfied with the condition of your gyroplane, he will sign it out to be test flown by a qualifed gyroplane pilot. **Pilots acceptable to conduct this test flight should be qualified gyroplane pilots with a minimum total experience of 70 hours flying, including 10 hours on gyroplanes of a similar type to the one on the test. They must also be in current flying practice with their log book endorsed with a valid certificate of experience.**

*Author and Gyroplane pilot Dave Organ preparing to take to the skies in his modified **Campbell Cricket**. About 47 Crickets were built between 1969 and 1971 by **Campbell Aircraft Ltd.**, based at Membury airfield near Newbury in Berkshire. All were originally powered by 1600cc. Volkswagen engines turning a 52" diameter wooden propeller and with 22ft diameter aluminium rotor blades. Many were later modified by uprating the engine to 1835cc. and replacing the Solex carburretors with 2 x twin choke Webers. Cruising airspeed is around 55 knots and its range is in the region of 1 hour and 50 minutes using the standard 7 gallon fuel tank. More recently, the original designer has introduced several new Mk's of the Cricket and it remains to be seen whether they will become as popular as the original Mk 1.*

With the test flight proving satisfactory, the application form, flight test report and Inspector's report, plus the annual fee, can be posted off to the PFA engineering office. Hopefully, within a short period of time, you will have your **Permit to Fly** for another 12 months.

Documents needed for the operation of your Gyroplane are:

1. Certificate of Registration.

2. Airframe Log Book.

3. Engine Log Book.

4. Flying Log Book.

5. Flight Release Certificate.

6. Permit to Fly. (Certificate of Validity).

The Brooklands "Hornet" was developed by the late Ernie Brooks in the 1960's from an earlier prototype which flew in both England and France. Mast, axle and keel is of alloy tube joined together with a welded steel fitting and powered by a 1600cc Volkswagen engine - later uprated to 1834cc. An estimated 32 models of the "Hornet" and its brother the "Mosquito" were eventually produced.

## Insurance

At present, insurance cover is not a legal requirement, but it is obviously advisable to have. There are several Brokers and Underwriters in the aviation field who should be able to quote for your requirements; usually, owners opt for Third Party Cover only, as full "Hull Cover" premiums can be prohibitive. See **"Useful Addresses/Aviation Insurance"** at rear of this book for companies to contact. Typical premium at time of printing is £275.00 p.a. for £250,000 third party liability and £385.00 p.a. for £500,000 liabilility.

## Medical Certificate

All Gyroplane pilots and student pilots must be in possession of a valid CAA Approved medical certificate. This is now a much more straight-forward procedure than it used to be because it now only requires the approval of your local G.P. You can request the pink certificate from either the PFA or the CAA and then arrange an appointment to see your local doctor. If, after the examination he or she is satisfied with your condition, he/she will sign and stamp the certificate, you pay the appropriate fee and you will then be in possession of a CAA Approved medical certificate. Fees vary for this and are nearly always negotiable.

| **Period of Validity** | Aged under 40 | - | 5 years |
| --- | --- | --- | --- |
| | Aged 40 - 49 | - | 2 years |
| | Aged 50 - 69 | - | 1 year |
| | Aged 70 and over | - | 6 months |

*G-BIPI* the first Gyroplane produced by **Everett Autogyros**, *seen here in its new livery after being completely refurbished by Colin Reeves. It is powered by an 1835cc Volkswagen engine turning a 52" diameter wooden propeller, using Weber carburettors and with four specially made silencers that adequately cope with the noise problem. Rotors are the ever popular 22ft Rotordynes and the pre-rotator is of the gearbox and telescopic shaft type. Mainwheel spats give better aerodynamics and also compliment the style.*

*Everetts started producing these machines in 1986 after acquiring 3 Campbell Crickets plus some jigs and tools from the old Campbell Aircraft business that had, by then, been closed down. After making some changes i.e. uprating the 1600cc engines to 1835cc; by replacing the old Permali Rotor blades with Rotordynes and by fitting Weber carburettors instead of the old Solex's, they obtained A1 approval from the CAA to produce these machines as a bona-fide aircraft manufacturer. That meant that Gyroplanes were manufactured and sold ready to fly, complete with Permit and all the necessary paperwork done. Later, the Volkswagen engines were replaced with the Rotax 532 and 582 varieties of two cylinder, liquid cooled, 2 stroke engines and in all, about 50 aircraft were sold around the world before production ceased in the mid 1990's.*

Today, **Everetts** are still able to supply parts for their existing machines and at the time of this publication, they are re-applying to the CAA for their A1 manufacturers' approval to be re-instated. When this happens, they intend to produce at least 20 more Rotax powered Gyroplanes. For further details of the current situation they can be contacted at the address shown on the contact addresses page at rear of this book.

## Flying Clothing

Experience has taught Gyroplane pilots that it is a very wise investment to purchase a good quality thermal/ waterproof, one-piece flying suit. These can be worn over your normal everyday clothing and are available from a variety of aviation clothing suppliers so you have a wide choice of styles and colours etc. to choose from.

If you intend flying a single seat Gyroplane, then a motorcycle type helmet is compulsory equipment - it's up to you on style - some prefer the full face type, although they can restrict your range of vision or, the open face type with a flip-up vizor for better visibility. Before deciding on this, please read the chapter on **Radiotelephony.** If you are going to fly "non radio" then ear defenders are a must - the most popular being the foam plug type that expand into the ear cavity - do use them.

Always protect the body extremities well - by this I mean the hands and feet. Invest in a good quality pair of leather gloves and a comfortable pair of warm shoes or pumps. Whatever else you wear is your own choice so long as you are adequately protected from the elements. Please remember that even on a hot summers day, it can still be cold at altitude.

*Originally designed by the late Rex McCandless, probably more noted for his design of the "Featherbed" Norton racing frame, this machine was later produced as the W.H.E. Airbuggy by W.H. Ekin and the prototype flew in February 1973. The first production model was sold in October 1975 and three more in 1976 and 1977. Powered by a 75 hp Volkswagen engine, unique features include a 'V' belt reduction drive and a push-button starter.*

# *Roger  Savage*

## *Gyroplanes*

**The most comprehensive Gyroplane flight training available anywhere in the U.K.**

Train safely in unrestricted airspace with some of the most beautiful countryside around, from our two bases, **Carlisle Airport** and our own airfield at **Kirkbride on Solway.**

We have two **VPM M16s (Rotax 914 powered)** two-seat trainers currently available, plus an **RAF 2000 GTXse** for ab-initio flight training or conversions from **Microlight/PPL(H) or (A)**.
Single seat gyroplane training on all types is also available.
So, if you wish to complete your **PPL(Gyroplanes)** with the maximum of fun in the minimum of time - yet in a thoroughly friendly and professional atmosphere - then look no further.
Flight training is full-time, by the hour, day, week - or longer.
Concentrated residential courses are a speciality. All ground subjects, including aerodynamics, are catered for on site.

**Please call Roger on:**   **017684 83859 or mobile 07836 272033**
**E-mail at:**   **gyroplanes@rogersavage.co.uk**
**Visit our web site at:**   **www.rogersavage.co.uk**
**or North West Gyro Club at:**  **www.nwgyro.co.uk**

### ✳ **Accommodation can be arranged** ✳

# Chapter 6

# CAA Requirements for Training

Assuming that you now have your own Gyroplane, complete with permit to fly, have organised your medical and insurance cover and have kitted yourself out with flying apparel - what next? The Civil Aviation Authority Publication CAP 53 tells you what the training requirements are and the following extracts from it, should point you in the right direction.

**Private Pilot's Licence**

**GYROPLANES (PPL(G))**

## 1    LICENCE PRIVILEGES

1.1  The privileges of a PPL(G) are set out in Schedule 8 to the Air Navigation Order. The holder of the licence may fly as pilot-in-command (PIC) or co-pilot of a gyroplane of any of the types specified in the Aircraft Rating section of the licence, provided that the licence contains a valid Medical Certificate and a valid Aircraft Rating. The Aircraft Rating is valid if a current Certificate of Test (C of T) or Certificate of Experience (C of E) is included in the holder's personal flying log book for the types of gyroplane to be flown. The holder may not fly the gyroplane for the purposes of public transport or aerial work other than flying instruction, and may not receive any remuneration for his services as pilot on any flight except as provided in paragraph 1.2. He may fly gyroplanes by day and by night in accordance with the Visual Flight Rules but may not carry passengers by night.

1.2  If, in due course, gyroplanes are permitted or certificated to fly at night, in IMC, or in controlled airspace under Instrument Flight Rules, Night Ratings, IMC Ratings and Instrument Ratings will be made available. A pilot may carry passengers by night only if his licence includes a Night Rating. A pilot may fly in weather conditions worse than those specified in the privileges of the PPL(A) in Schedule 8 of the ANO, only if he holds an Instrument Meteorological Conditions (IMC) Rating or an Instrument Rating (IR(A)). In addition, the holder of a PPL(G) may give flying instruction if the licence includes an Assistant Flying or a Flying Instructor's Rating. In these circumstances, the licence holder may receive remuneration for giving flying instruction or conducting Flight Tests provided that he and the student are members of the same flying club. These additional ratings are described in subsequent chapters.

1.3 A licence valid for flight in gyroplanes is not valid for flight in helicopters, aeroplanes, balloons or airships.

## 2. AIRCRAFT RATING PRIVILEGES

2.1 The Aircraft Rating enables the licence holder to act as PIC of the specific types of gyroplane contained in the Aircraft Rating page of the licence.

2.2 The validity of Aircraft Rating privileges is maintained by inclusion in the pilot's personal flying log book of periodic Cs of T or Cs of E. Details of the requirements to be met for the inclusion of a C of T or C of E and the periods of their validity are given in Part 1, Appendix H.

## 3. MEDICAL REQUIREMENTS

3.1 An applicant for a PPL(G) must hold a valid **CAA Approved Medical Certificate.**

3.2 Information on the arrangements to obtain a Medical Certificate, the medical requirements and periods of validity are given in Part 1, Chapter 2.

## 4. FLYING EXPERIENCE REQUIREMENTS

4.1 An applicant for a PPL(G) shall produce evidence of having satisfactorily completed a course of flying training with a gyroplane flying instructor, to a syllabus recognised by the Authority. The applicant must also successfully complete a Flight Test, under the supervision of an authorised Gyroplane Examiner.

4.2 The syllabus of flying training must provide for a minimum of **40 hours** as pilot of a flying machine; this must include at least:

(a) 10 hours dual instruction in a 2 seat Gyroplane.

(b) 10 hours supervised solo in a single or 2 seat Gyroplane.

(c) 10 hours as PIC of the first type of gyroplane to be included in the licence, no less than 3 hours of which must be as PIC on cross-country flights, including at least 2 flights to an aerodrome not less than 25 nm from the departure aerodrome gained within 9 months of the date of the application for the licence.

NOTE: On the 40 hour course for ab-initio students, **5 hours** instruction in an approved 2 seat Gyro glider can also be included.

*A Bensen/Cricket Hybred powered by an Arrow 500 GT air cooled 2-stroke engine*

## 5.   FLIGHT TEST (GYROPLANES)

5.1   An applicant for a PPL(G) will be required to complete successfully a Flight Test conducted or supervised by an authorised Gyroplane Examiner.

5.2   The Flight Test will cover the manoeuvres and drills detailed in Part 3, Appendix C.

### 5.3   **Flight Test Pass Conditions**

The whole of the Flight Test must be completed within a period of 28 days. A candidate who fails in any part of the Flight Test may be required to undertake further flying training before being accepted for a retest.

# 6.  GROUND EXAMINATIONS

An applicant for a PPL(G) will be required to pass the Ground Examination in each of the following subjects:

(a) Aviation Law, Flight Rules and Procedures as detailed in Part 2, Appendix C;

(b) Navigation to PPL 'A' Standard;

(c) Meteorology to PPL 'A' Standard;

(d) Aircraft (relevant to gyroplanes);

(e) Aircraft (Type);

(f) Human performance and limitations.

Examinations in subjects (a), (b), (c), (d) and (f) are written multiple-choice papers with a minimum pass mark of 70%; examination (e) is an oral examination conducted by the gyroplane Examiner supervising the Flight Test, on the type of gyroplane used on the Flight Test. A valid pass in the written examinations must be obtained in the 12 months preceding the date of application for the licence.

# 7.  THE LICENCE

7.1  When the PPL(G) is issued, it will be endorsed with:

"The holder of this licence is not permitted to fly gyroplanes out of sight of the surface or by sole reference to instruments."

7.2  The requirements for the revalidation of the Aircraft Rating in the PPL(G) are detailed in Part 1, Appendix H.

# 8.  EXEMPTIONS FROM FLYING TRAINING AND GROUND EXAMINATIONS

8.1  Experienced pilots who wish to claim exemption from any of the licensing requirements should apply to the Authority (FCL4) for an assessment of their experience.

## 8.2 Exemptions from Flying Training

8.2.1    A holder of PPL(A), PPL(A) Microlight (2 seat '3-axis'), PPL(H), PPL(A) SLMG will normally be exempt from completing the training at paragraph 4.2(a).

8.2.2 In the case of the holder of a PPL(A) Microlight, with no operational limitations, the flying experience required at paragraph 4.2(a) may be reduced to 6 hours if previous experience has been gained on weight-shift microlights.

8.2.3 A holder of gliding qualifications will normally be exempt the training at paragraph 4.2(a), provided he already has the aeroplane flying experience for the issue of a PPL(A) Group A, detailed at Part 2, appendix D.

## 8.3 Exemptions from Ground Examinations

A holder of a valid PPL(A) (except a PPL(A) Microlight) or a PPL(H), will normally be exempt from the ground examinations at paragraphs 6(a), (b), (c) and (f).

## 8.4 Professional Pilot's Licence

The holder of a Professional Pilot's Licence (Aeroplanes or Helicopters) will normally be entitled to the exemptions at paragraphs 8.2 and 8.3 appropriate to the private privileges contained within his professional licence.

## 9.    FLIGHT TEST AND GROUND EXAMINATIONS - VALIDITY PERIODS

The Flight Test and Ground Examinations required for the issue of a PPL(G) must be completed within the periods of time shown below before the date of application:

(a)                        Ground Examinations - 12 months

(b)                        Flight Test - 9 months.

# 10. APPLICATIONS

An application for the issue of a PPL(G) should include:

(a) Personal Flying Log Book;

(b) Medical Certificate;

(c) Form FCL 102B;

(d) Qualifying Cross-Country Certificates;

(e) Any other relevant Flight Crew Licence, Rating or Letter of Assessment;

(f) Prescribed Charge.

If, after reading the previous pages, you are still in doubt as to your own particular requirements, do as advised and contact the CAA (FCL 4) for an assessment.

Contact your choice of instructor and co-ordinate with him or her on dates, times venues, etc., and when appointments are made, do your best to honour them. Turn up for instruction with all your kit including clothing, maps, log books, "Permit to Fly", fuel and above all, an airworthy Gyroplane. Make sure you arrange insurance-cover for the instructor to fly it as well - He may need to assess its capability before you attempt it yourself.

When you have completed the course including the ground subjects, a general flight test (GFT) will have to be taken in conjunction with a CAA Approved Examiner. Some instructors are also examiners so you could complete the whole course and G.F.T. with one person.

After a successful G.F.T., the examiner will sign out your flying log book to that effect and you can immediately apply to the CAA for your PPL(G).

Being the proud owner of a PPL(G) is in itself, a great achievement, but please understand that the learning process has only just begun. If you use common

Photo: Roger Savage

This Montgomerie-Merlin is one of a pair of Gyroplanes that have recently been converted by Mike Mee from Rotax 582 to 912 power. Mike obviously looks pleased with the results and says that the machine is now capable of a 300-mile range (double that of the original engine) with a slightly improved cruise speed of around 80 mph. - Photo: Roger Savage

sense and take it easy on your first few flights, the gyroplane will eventually feel part of you and confidence will increase. Do stay away from built-up areas, woods, lakes or power cables - these could restrict your choice of landing area if you have to put your machine down quickly.

Should you be unfortunate enough to suffer an engine failure, the gyroplane will start to descend immediately. This will inevitably draw on your training experience with power-off landings and it certainly helps if you have a little plot of green below in which o put down safely. Many aircraft accidents occur through running out of fuel, so know your machine's fuel consumption rate and have at least 1½gallons safety margin on cross country flights.

Don't forget the pre-flight inspection before take-off, always ensure you have enough take-off space when operating out of a farm strip or field and that there are no obstructions at the end of the take-off run - you may need all the space you can get. Remember also that on a calm day, the take-off run could be as much as 300 yards, even with a pre-spin.

## British Rotorcraft Association

This Association was formed in 1990 by the amalgamation of several nationwide Gyroplane "struts" that operated within the **Popular Flying Association.** Their aim was to become the U. K. Representative Gyroplane body that could oversee the activities of the Gyroplane movement and represent the interests of its members more closely. The objectives of the association are primarily to promote, support and encourage Gyroplane construction and flying and to liaise with both the PFA and CAA on matters of safety, training, engineering and licencing. Members receive a regular newsletter giving up-to-date help and advice and several fly-ins or rallies are held each year at different venues throughout the UK.

At the time of publication, moves are afoot by the current Committee to link the Gyroplane movement more closely to the PFA. If this move goes ahead, the new organisation will be known as **"The British Gyroplane Squadron"** of the PFA - "Squadron" being the term used to encompass national special interest groups.

Whatever name the Gyroplane movement agrees to use, the aims and objectives would remain unchanged and all Gyroplane enthusiasts whether they be flyers or not, should be encouraged to become-members - after all, it is an organisation run by Gyroplane enthusiasts for Gyroplane enthusiasts.

# Chapter 7
# Gyroplane Alternatives & Options

The following information gives the general state of approved alternatives for single seat gyroplanes avail‑able at the time of going to press; others could possibly be pending - if in doubt, contact your Gyroplane Inspector or the PFA Engineering Department.

| TYPE | ENGINE | ROTORS | PROPELLER | AIRFRAME |
|---|---|---|---|---|
| **Bensen** | **McCulloch** 72 and 90h.p. **Volkswagen** 1600 and 1834 cc **Rotax** 503 532, 582, **Arrow** G.T.500 | Bensen H-R Permali Rotorhawk Rotordyne Dragon Wings | For **McCulloch** & **Volkswagen** 2 blade Bensen Troyer, Fern Permali, Lodge. For **Rotax** 3 blade GSC, Warp Drive, Kodiak. Ivo-Prop | 6061-T6 or HE30 TF 2"x2" Alloy Tubing Mast - 2 pieces 2"x1". (Redundant) |
| **Campbell Cricket** | **Volkswagen** 1600cc and 1834cc. **Rotax** 503, 532, 582 **Arrow** G.T.500 | As for Bensen | As for Bensen | Originals of special die produced 2"x2" tubing otherwise as for Bensen |
| **Everett** | **Volkswagen** 1834cc **Rotax** 582 | As for Bensen | As for Bensen | As for Bensen |
| **Montgomerie** | **Rotax** 532 & 582 **Rotax** 912 | As for Bensen | 3 blade GSC 52" & 60" Ivo-Prop Arplast for 912 conversion. | As for Bensen |
| **Ken Brock (KB-2)** | **Rotax** 582 | As for Bensen | 3 blade GSC 52" Ivo-Prop | As for Bensen |
| **Brooklands Hornet and Mosquito** | **Volkswagen** 1600cc and 1834cc | As for Bensen | As for Bensen | Alloy tube secured with welded and brazed steel fittings bolted to mast, keel and axle. |
| **W.H.E. Airbuggy** | Volkswagen 1600cc and 1834cc. | As for Bensen | Hoffman 2 blade metal | Welded steel tube T45 and T26 |

# Chapter 8

# Powerplant Options
## For Single Seat Gyroplanes

Rotax 582 64 H.P. dual ignition, 2 cylinder liquid cooled 2-stroke. Optional equipment includes electric starter, oil injection and alternative ratio gearbox.

Arrow GT 500R 65 H.P. 2 cylinder air cooled 2-stroke. Includes electric starter motor and alternator. Optional equipment includes an epicyclic gearbox and dual ignition.

Volkswagen 1600 or 1834 cc 55-70 H.P. 4 cylinder air cooled 4-stroke. Available complete or self build. Optional equipment includes belt reduction unit, starter motor unit and dual Weber carburettors.

As mentioned earlier, **Mike Mee** has transformed his Montgomerie Merlin Gyroplane by transplanting it with a Rotax 912 engine and he says that another similar machine has now been done as well. One of the main design criteria was to bring the new engine's thrust line closer to the machine's centre of gravity - in line with the research findings of the **University of Glasgow**. This took some trouble to achieve but from the original difference of 2.50", Mike reduced it to just 0.625". All technical data regarding this was originally handled by the CAA with Roger Savage acting as the liaison man and who did all the flight testing at Carlisle Airport. It is hoped that the PFA will eventually oversee any future conversions and Mike is still looking into this possibility. The end result of all Mike's efforts is a single seat Gyroplane, capable of a 300 mile range, or endurance of 2 hours and 40 minutes with a reserve of about 30 minutes - a serious cross-country machine.

**Technical Data:**

| | |
|---|---|
| **Empty weight:** | 355 lbs, |
| **Rate of Climb:** | 1000 ft. per minute, |
| **Fuel capacity:** | 10 gallons, |
| **Fuel consumption:** | 3 gallons per hour, |
| **Cruise speed:** | 75 - 80 m.p.h., |
| **Propeller:** | 60" diameter, 3 bladed, ground adjustable, |
| **Rotors:** | 22 foot Dragon Wings. |

Rotax 503; a 50 hp air cooled (force fed fan), 2 cylinder, 2-stroke engine, turning a 50" diameter, 3 bladed, G.S.C. propeller. This installation is on a plans-built Campbell Cricket.

Subaru EA 81 - 1800cc and EA 82 - 2200cc, liquid cooled, Flat four engine complete with Belt Reduction drive unit, Starter and Alternator - installed here in an RAF 2000.

# Chapter 9

# Two Seat Training Gyroplanes

## The Canadian RAF 2000 GTXse

This 2 seater (side by side) Gyroplane is the latest model from the Rotary Air Force company in Saskatchewan, Canada and is now a very popular choice for both serious cross-country flying and for training purposes. The fully enclosed cockpit is fitted with dual controls, is luxuriously fitted out with carpet and heating and the doors are removable if the weather so permits.

Powered by a Subaru 2200cc liquid cooled Legacy engine of 130h.p., coupled to a 2.1:1 belt reduction drive unit, this aircraft has a flight duration of 3.5 hours at a cruise speed of between 70 and 75 m.p.h. Fuel usage is 5.25 gallons per hour and the climb rate is 1000 feet per minute (2 persons aboard).

Standard features include an adjustable mast for changing the centre of gravity of the aircraft, 30ft diameter rotor blades, composite 3 blade, adjustable, 68" diameter propeller, rotor pre-spin, rotor brake, pitch and roll trimmer, plus full flying and engine instruments.

This particular machine which incorporates twin fuel pumps and hydraulic main wheel brakes is owned and operated by **Mr Mike Goldring, from Newton Abbott, Devon, the sole U.K importer for the RAF 2000.**

**RAF 2000 GTXse** instrument panel shows the standard flight instruments plus an array of add-on items such as:- **Skyforce G.P.S., transponder and altitude encoder, Icom transceiver and intercom, full circuit breaker board for nav. lights, panel and strobes etc., plus fuel pressure warning lights.**

# The Italian VPM M16

2 seater tandem is another Gyroplane used for training purposes. Originally powered by an Arrow 4 cylinder, 2-stroke air cooled engine, this one has been converted to a Rotax 914, 4 cylinder, 4-stroke air cooled turbocharged engine. It has dual controls, a hydraulic pre-rotator and carbon fibre rotor blades. **G-BUZL** is owned and operated by Roger Savage, seen here on a training sortie with a student pilot. Roger and co-engineer Mike Mee were both instrumental in the design and fitting of this conversion to **G-BUZL** and Roger says that the turbocharged 914 has transformed the M16 into the most fantastic dual seat training aircraft. The engine is a dream to handle and the power is comparatively quiet and very smooth, making the students feel immediately at ease with the aircraft. The VPM and the Rotax 914 engine is proving both economical and tremendous fun to fly.

# Chapter 10

# Rotor Theory and Handling

## by John C. Kitchin

Because of the absolute necessity to avoid negative 'g', the gyroplane is not aerobatic This does not mean that turbulence is a danger, for the gyroplane 'slices' through the up and down currents, giving a much smoother ride on a bumpy day than a fixed-wing aircraft of similar weight. The rotor blades are only about 7½" wide, rotating at about 350 rpm, so any thermal is 'sampled', giving a noticeable reduction in its effect.

We should, before further considerations, get to know how the rotor blade works Once you understand this, the 'flight envelope' becomes simple and logical.

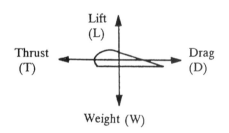

This may be our usual idea of the forces acting on an aerofoil section.

Actually it's misleading.

In fact, the Lift vector is tilted forwards. If it were not, the gyroplane couldn't fly.

This forward-leaning tendency can be divided into two vectors, upwards and forwards thus:

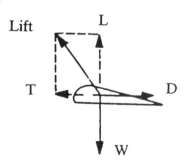

This exaggerated diagram illustrates the stable state, when the forward vector of the lift equals the drag and the upward vector of the lift equals the weight.

You can see that if the Weight increases, the Lift must increase which, in turn, produces a larger forward vector 'T'. You would expect the rotor revs to increase - which indeed they do - quite automatically, until 'D' builds up and the rotor is once again in a stable condition. If the Weight decreases, less Lift is required but Drag is still large, so the rotor slows down.

Some gyroplanes need to have their rotors started by hand and it is necessary to learn how best to accelerate the rotor, depending on the existing wind. When it is stopped, or rotating slowly, it tends to flap as the 'into-wind' blade sails up. This has been known to cause the rearmost blade to flex and hit the ground; an expensive exercise. In this state, you must be gentle with the rotor and not allow too much wind through the 'disc'. The blades stiffen through centrifugal force and begin to develop lift. This gradual build-up of rotor revs is achieved by taxying slowly into a light breeze or, in a strong wind, must be achieved by tilting the rotor disc forwards, to spill some of the air that would otherwise pass through it. The ideal wind, passing through the disc, will supply sufficient energy to overcome the inherent inertia of the rotor, so that it accelerates continuously until it reaches flying rpm.

You may feel that this is complicated but a little practice is all you need. If you dash off into wind too fast, the rotor flexes and the control column bangs forward and back against its rear stop as the blades pound their 'teeter stops'. This is **very** bad for the machinery and considerably extends your take-off run. A competent gyroplane pilot should be able to take off in under 300 yards with no wind. With a 20kt breeze he's probably airborne in about 75.

Teeter stops physically prevent the blades from rocking too far. The blades are permitted to rock about their 'teeter-bolt', so that, as they rotate, the advancing blade (which would otherwise produce more lift than the retreating blade) is allowed to fly up. The retreating blade simultaneously moves downwards as it rotates. This 'give and take' alters the relative airflow over the blades, to decrease the angle of attack on the advancing blade and increase the angle of attach on the retreating blade, so that the overall lift across the rotor remains, effectively, constant in the roll plane. If the blade couldn't 'teeter', the gyroplane would suffer considerable vibration and would roll to the left.

Another consideration of the rotor is its efficiency at pruning trees, hedges and, above all, people, if the pilot gets too close to obstacles. People approaching the gyroplane, when the blades are turning, must be well briefed to approach from the front, where the path of the blades is highest.

How on earth does one control a 21ft diameter rotor? It's quite simple really - the rotor blades are **flown** to their new position as requested by the control column. There is a small lag between the control input and the required response which often, in the early stages of training, leads to overcontrolling. One grandmother, in the early stages with the gyro-glider, nearly made me airsick by frantic overcontrolling on the 'ailerons'. We rocked our way over the runway, until I just <u>had</u> to take over. Some light aircraft pilots, who are used to more 'positive' controls, have to learn to <u>ease</u> the stick in the required direction. Pupils soon learn to 'suggest' rather than to 'instruct' control inputs. One of the demonstrations, on the gyro-glider, is quickly to wiggle the stick in all directions from the central position; the glider continues straight on. This comes about because the control inputs are applied to the rotor blades 90° before the required new position of the rotor disc. A diagram will help to illustrate a pitch change:

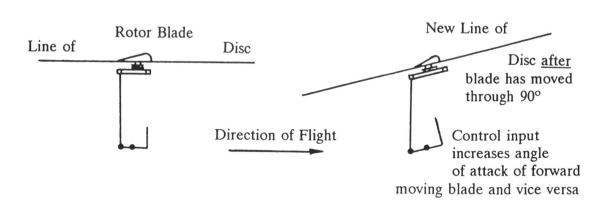

You can see that 'back' on the stick equates with 'up elevator' and vice versa. Left stick gives 'left aileron' and vice versa. Just like an ordinary aeroplane.

If then, a gyroplane handles like a fixed-wing aircraft, why do people bother to fly them? Mostly for fun. They are as cheap as any other light aircraft to fly, with no heavy maintenance costs. They look different; a 'one-upmanship' point. A gyroplane can be stopped after a landing run of only 5 yards and needs between 200 and 300 yards for take off. It can be stored in a long garage needing 22 feet by less than 6 feet. It has no car-like cabin, but sits you out in the wind, (and rain!) very like an aerial motorbike, with visibility to match. Two cylinder Rotax powered gyroplanes use in the region of 20-27 litres/hour of fuel while the Volkswagen uses around 14-16 litres/hour. The usual cruising speed is 50 to 55 kts; a cross-country needs care, if it is at all windy, for the direction of flight has a very considerable effect on groundspeed.

A gyroplane cannot stall; this was one of the reasons for its development in the '20s and '30s. The rotor revs are constant when it is carrying a given weight. If you slow down below about 25 kts, the gyroplane starts to sink, even with full power on, in a high nose up attitude. When the airspeed indicator reads zero, you will be 'mushing' downwards at about 12 kts vertically, faster without power. To recover, ease the stick forward and regain indicated airspeed to above 25 kts and by adding the appropriate amount of power, you will be flying level again.

At the top end of the flight envelope, placarded at 80 kts or thereabouts, and limited to 80 kts by the CAA since the 1970 accident at Farnborough, the controls are very crisp.

Here we sometimes have problems with P.I.O. (Pilot Induced Oscillation); our old friend from initial training flights. The slight lag between control input and its effect, is still there, of course. There is still the tendency to, as it were, 'add a bit for Mum' rather than to ease in control inputs. At these higher speeds, a small input has a larger effect, so PIO, or overcontrolling, must be watched for. Should it occur, just slow down a bit and let the machine catch you up.

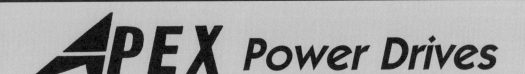

# Chapter 11

# Sleeping Projects

## The Wombat Gyroplane

One British Gyroplane that didn't quite make it as a runaway success is this stylish looking **Wombat Gyroplane**, the brainchild of veteran Gyroplane guru **Chris Julian** from Cornwall. Chris, who had at least 25 years experience building, flying and training on Gyroplanes, decided in the late 1980's, to combine all his ideas into one concept Gyroplane. This eventually evolved to become the

**Wombat**, a very well engineered design that many people believed to be years ahead of its time.

The PFA had taken this design under its wing, and in order to comply with the requirements of Section T, had agreed with Chris a flight test programme to evaluate safety and performance parameters. He had been forging ahead with this and test results looked very promising when the unthinkable happened - on the 17th May 1997, Chris sadly died in an unrelated air accident.

It would have been a nice tribute to Chris for us to see the fruits of his labours come to fruition, with the Wombat to be in current production, but alas, no one took up the challenge and the project was abandoned. However, there are rumours that we may not have seen the last of this exceptional machine. For the records, the **Wombat** was designed primarily out of round section alloy tube and powered by a Rotax 582 liquid cooled engine turning a 60" diameter 3 bladed GSC propeller. It had a semi-enclosed fibreglass nacelle, nosewheel suspension, a nosewheel brake and the rotors were 22ft diameter Rotordynes.

**Unconfirmed performance figures are:**

| | |
|---|---|
| **Rate of climb** | 1000ft per minute +; |
| **Cruise speed** | 80 mph+; |
| **Vne.** | 100mph; |
| **Empty weight** | 270lbs; |
| **Fuel tank capacity** | 17 gallons; |
| **Fuel consumption** | 3.5 - 4 gallons per hour. |

*Chris Julian flying his Wombat over Wadebridge Wind Farm - photo-Shirley Jennings*

# Concept Twin Touring Autogyro

From the Montgomerie stable comes this unique two seat tandem, fully enclosed design based on the combination of the very successful Merlin single seat gyroplane and the open style two seat Parsons machine. Those who are familiar with both of these types will at once see the similarities - it is a stretched version of both. Merlin features include the exposed keel and the rudder/tailplane unit while the Parsons features include the now familiar twin masts and the tandem seating arrangement. The powerplant is a Subaru 2200cc engine with a reduction gearbox driving a five bladed, ground adjustable, GSC wooden propeller.

It is anticipated that future development changes will take place and these will include an engine change to a turbo-charged Rotax 914; raising the keel and introducing a retractable front wheel strut; moving the tailplane unit about 8" rearwards for better yaw control and replacing the flat formed perspex canopy sheets with a styled moulded version.

This Autogyro is intended to be a serious touring aircraft with front joystick only but it could easily be converted to dual control for use as a training machine if needed. A factory spokesman said that it is a long term project due to the slow and expensive design proving system that exists in this country but is hopeful that it will fly within the next few years!!

# Concept Fandango

This aircraft made its debut at the 1996 PFA Rally at Cranfield and its somewhat unorthodox style created quite a stir. The creation of Colchester based **Dan Watts**, this fully enclosed 2 seat machine is powered by two Rotax 532 engines coupled together by means of belts, pulleys and sprag clutches. The final thrust is via a 1200mm diameter ducted fan which produces 600lbs of static thrust. It has a unique patented rotor head, a hydraulic pre-rotator and a steerable tailwheel.

Some ground testing has taken place but to date no specific details are forthcoming - the CAA are still considering its possibilities. The gross weight is around 1200lbs and although rotor blades have not as yet been sourced, it is thought they would require to be around 30 feet in diameter with a 9" chord.

# Chapter 12

# Why does a Gyroplane Porpoise?

## by John C. Kitchin

Imagine a gyroplane in fast level flight. The stick is pulled back. Up comes the nose and the disc of the rotor is inclined further backwards. Rotor drag increases, tending to pull back the top of the mast and thus pulling up the nose. Yet more drag is caused by the rotor so the nose comes even higher. We are actually talking about small amounts here but, if it is allowed to continue, the nose will come up so far that either the pilot will want to push forward on the stick or, with the nose very high in the air, the airspeed will decay and the craft will mush downwards well behind the drag curve. If he does push the stick forwards he will enter a dive, airspeed and control sensitivity will again increase and he may well pull out into another zoom climb. He is set up for a divergent oscillation in pitch.

In the nose high position the thrust will be having an effect on his apparent weight, or 'g'. As rotor rpm are proportional to the square root of weight, and the vertical component of thrust is reducing this weight (as is the rapidly reducing airspeed), there will be a decrease in rotor rpm. If he falls back into a mush then this does not matter as the rpm will be restored once he settles into the descent, power on or off. All power will do now is to alter the nose up angle of the machine and the rate of descent.

Let us assume the worst case now. The pilot has allowed the nose to rise way up and his airspeed is falling rapidly. He now pushes hard forwards on the stick and has enough airspeed to effect a rapid rotation into the nose down position. As he does this his weight, as far as the rotor is concerned, will decrease. At ¼ 'g' (¼ normal weight) the rotor will stabilise at half its usual rpm. It will drop from 360 to 180! At this figure of 'g' the rate of slowing of the rotor is at its maximum and it does not take more than a few seconds for this rpm drop to occur. At low rpm the rotor blades can and will flex. We are then concerned with the inherent rigidity of the blades, for they are not being held properly in place (coned upwards) by centrifugal force, and the clearance between the drooping blades and the fin or the propeller. If this is not enough then we are in trouble, for if the blades strike the fin they will either slow down even more or perhaps break. Violent blade sailing will certainly occur as the airspeed increases again with the rotor rpm this low. If, on starting the zoom climb, the pilot had applied stick to set a climb attitude and then held the nose in that position there would be no trouble. Alternatively he could have taken off power and entered the mush that much earlier - or just slowed down and eased the craft into level flight. If, in a steep climb, you feel yourself getting weightless roll into a turn and increase 'g' this way. If, in a power dive, the airspeed gets high then expect a tendency for the nose to rise further than you anticipate when you ease back a little on the stick. Either stop it by a forward jab, or merely slow down.

The wrong thing to do is to overcontrol. This is the basic cause of the so-called porpoise. It is, as far as I can determine, totally avoidable if you insist on flying the machine rather than allowing it to fly you.

Finally, a word of warning. Some years ago a student training manual (similar to the Bensen handbook) was produced. It was suggested that the CAA should approve this to cut out personal tuition. The CAA considered this and rejected it completely. There is absolutely no substitute for personal tuition where you progress as fast (and as safely) as possible. Read the handbook and have a go on your own and the odds are that you'll bend, not usually yourself, but certainly your machine. It has happened too often, is expensive and unnecessary.

# Chapter 13

# Radiotelephony

*The Lynx Micro System*

Today, with ever increasing air traffic, most British airfields and airports insist on aircraft having two-way radio communication if flying within the limits of their boundaries. **Radiotelephony (RTF)** is essential for the safe operation of aircraft in a busy environment. It enables you to obtain airfield information and instructions relating to the safe movement of air traffic and allows you to communicate your way through busy air traffic zones, whether they be civil or military.

Radio waves are not confined by national boundaries and for this reason radio is regulated on an international basis. In the UK the primary legislation is the **Wireless Telegraphy Act 1949 (the WT Act)**. This act empowers the Secretary of State to make and enforce regulations regarding the installation and use of radio, including the requirements to be met by users, manufacturers and importers of any radio equipment that is capable of causing radio interference.

In the case of aeronautical radio stations, the responsibility for the issue of operator licences and the approval of the equipment and its installation is delegated to the **Civil Aviation Authority**. Regulations regarding the operation of aircraft radio equipment and aeronautical radio stations are contained in the **Air Navigation Order 1995 (ANO)** Articles 15, 21, 41, 93 and schedule 8. Any Aircraft that uses radio, whether installed or non-installed (portable), requires an Aircraft Radio Licence issued by the **Radiocommunications Agency (RA).**

Aircraft **VHF** radio communications equipment operates in the band 118.00 MHz to 136.975 MHz. Individual frequencies are allocated every 25 KHz giving rise to 760 channels. Some older radios may have 720 or even 360 channels with an upper limit of 135.975 MHz. Radio equipment is designed with a minimum number of controls. The operating frequency is selected by rotary knobs or switches, allowing the frequency to be adjusted in steps of 1 MHz, 100 KHz and either 50 or 25 KHz.

All too often the receiver VOLUME and SQUELCH controls may be incorrectly set. SQUELCH is an electronic switch that mutes the receiver audio output when no signal is received. This facility is designed to reduce operator fatigue which can result from continuous exposure to white noise. The correct setting procedure for the SQUELCH control is:

Current model ICOM Radios. The IC-A3E and the IC - A22E

1 )     Set the volume control to approximately halfway;

2)      Turn the SQUELCH control up until a hiss appears, this is background noise;

3)      Turn back the SQELCH control until the hiss just stops, this occurs quite abruptly;

4)      Leave the SQUELCH control in this position.

Apart from student pilots under training, operators of radio equipment must be in possession of a **Flight Radiotelephony Operator's Licence (FRTOL).** This entitles you to operate the radio communications equipment in any aircraft, whether it be a fixed installation or a portable unit. If you don't already hold an **FRTOL**, the best route to obtaining one is to join a local flying school or Microlight club. Most of them have the facilities and staff to see you through the syllabus and of course to examine you afterwards.

Once you've acquired this licence, it is for life - there are no further exams or tests to undertake, although it must be said that it is important to be aware of current changes in RT procedure - it does happen from time to time. As a direct result of the 1977 Tenerife accident involving two Boeing 747's, **RTF phraseology** was modified to avoid any ambiguity or confusion and has been progressively modified over the intervening years so, the advice is to keep up-to-date. The correct phraseology is detailed in CAP 413 Radiotelephony Manual.

Choosing the right type of equipment for use in a Gyroplane is not a great problem. Generally speaking, most installations are of the portable type and the type now acknowledged as the market standard is the **ICOM handheld VHF transceiver**. It is quite a compact unit measuring 170x60x35mm excluding the short aerial and can quite easily be accommodated in the cockpit area within easy operating distance.

Two models are available - the **IC-A3E** and the **IC-A22E**. The former is the most popular, having a 760 channel com. system only, whereas the latter also includes a 200 channel navigation system. Both come complete with their own charging system and headset adapter and the cost varies, depending on the supplier but ranges between £250.00 and £325.00, plus the inevitable VAT.

For improved **RT** reception, it would be advisable to install a **remote aerial**, sited as far away from engine interference as is possible. The earthing plate or ground plane should be approximately 250mm square and be of a suitable light and thin alloy. Aerial suppliers include a strip of glue-backed alloy tape about 50mm wide in their kit and this can be applied inside the nacelle or cockpit area. It is arranged in a cross or star pattern and the aerial positioned down through its centre and secured with the earthing nut.

*Cockpit layout on an Everett Gyroplane. Note the ICOM Radio Installation and the very prominent G.P.S.*

**Headsets and helmets** are a personal choice but if you are intending to fly an open cockpit Gyroplane, you will need a helmet which incorporates a headset as well. There are currently several types to choose from - the **Lynx Micro** system, the **Comunica Beta Plus** system and the **Ultra-Pro** system to name but a few. All have had the benefit of years of experience and testing, especially in the microlight world, so it really is your personal choice. All types have noise attenuating headsets that provide hearing protection in noise levels up to 110dB, a noise cancelling microphone and are fully compatible with all available radio transceivers. Ancillary equipment such as visors, press to talk switches (PTT) and certain adapters are all available at extra cost.

*The Comunica Beta Plus System*

# Chapter 14

# Projects from Abroad

## The U.F.O. Heli-Thruster

This aircraft was designed and developed over a period of nine years by Mac Gillespie from New Zealand and it first flew in December 1997. It is a roomy two seat Gyroplane with a fibreglass body built over an alloy frame. Powered by either a Subaru 1800 or 2200 Legacy engine and sporting 28ft rotors, it boasts a cruise speed of around 100mph and a climb rate of  1500ft/minute, (one person aboard + 9 gallons of fuel) - fuel capacity is 22 gallons (100 litres). The really impressive thing that strikes you when looking at this machine is its aerodynamic appeal and Mac Gillespie emphasises this as a major factor in its design parameters - the body shape is a unique teardrop style, tested in a wind tunnel to create the final shape and the head and keel shrouds are detachable. The tricycle undercarriage has nosewheel suspension only and the mainwheel struts are aerodynamically streamlined.

The tall tail is again, specially designed and its horizontal stabiliser can be trimmed to allow for variations in location of the Subaru reduction box. Although this aircraft is  not available in the UK yet, the Agent is offering to sell the major parts in kit form with a promise of other components in the near future. Of course, if it does appear in this country, then the CAA will obviously take it under their wing before it will be allowed to fly legally - we await further developments. In the meantime, for further details contact:- **Mr Graham Kelly - mobile no. 0709-2337612.**

# The Hawk 4 Gyroplane

This much heralded aircraft has been developed and manufactured by the Groen Brothers Aviation inc., from Salt Lake City, Utah, USA. It is a genuine 4-seater aircraft with the ability to take off vertically and boasts a cruise range of 420 miles. The body is of aluminium stressed skin over a semi monocoque frame and the

powerplant is a Teledyne Continental 350 h.p.engine. It has a 3-bladed propeller and a 2-bladed rotor system, 42 ft. in diameter.

**Performance figures are:**

| | |
|---|---|
| **Rate of climb** | 1500 ft./minute. |
| **Max. speed at 12,000 ft.** | 150 m.p.h. |
| **Cruise speed at 12,000 ft**. | 130 m.p.h. |
| **Service ceiling** | 16,000ft |
| **Max. gross weight** | 2,800lbs |
| **Useful load** | 960lbs |

Derivatives of this Type include an Airborne Law Enforcement version, an Air Surveillance version and a Crop Spraying version.

Further information is available from:- **Groen Brothers Aviation Inc., 2640 West California Avenue, Suite A, Salt Lake City, Utah 84104-4593 U.S.A. Tel. (801)973-0177 Fax.(801)973-4027 or visit their web site at www.gbagyros.com**

# Dominator Gyroplane

Another machine from across the pond is the single seat open frame **Dominator Gyroplane**, developed and flown for a few years now but still a popular machine in spite of it's unorthadox look. Allegedly, the first gyroplane to incorporate both the **Tall Tail** and the **Centre of Gravity thrust line**, this may be the way Gyroplane design will go in the future (the latest Air Command being just one example - see page 77 ). Built from 2"x 2" alloy tubing, full suspension landing gear with 9" travel, tall tail and horizontal stabiliser, this machine, powered by a 50hp Rotax 503 turning a 3 bladed, 60" diameter propeller, boasts a top speed of 90 mph. and a cruise speed of 45-50 mph.

Photo: Larry Gleason

The rotor blades are the now popular **Dragon Wings** rotors which are made of all aluminium with bonded skins and are 23.5ft diameter with a 7" chord. This Gyroplane can apparently be built from plans but will need to be clarified with the CAA first before embarking on any build project here in the UK. Further details are available from: **Rotor Flight Dynamics, Inc., 19242 Grange Hall Loop, Lithia, FL33547, USA Tel (813) 634-3370, Fax (813) 633-3296.**

# Chapter 15

# Pre-Rotators

Pre-rotators, pre-spins or spin ups are all references to a mechanical or hydraulic means of initiating the rotation of the rotor blades prior to take off. This has its maximum benefit in calm or light wind conditions and enables the gyroplane to lift off within a shorter ground run that would otherwise be possible. Power for this is tapped off the engine via a friction drive mechanism which is operated by a simple hand lever.

It is very important to stress that before making use of a pre-rotator, it is essential that the gyroplane pilot is fully conversant with rotor technique and is capable of **manually** controlling rotor blade speeds, both before and after flight. It is of little use lining up on the airstrip, winding up the pre-rotator and dashing off at goodness knows what speed, hoping that the poor gyroplane will quickly become airborne. Eventually it will of course but it is courting disaster to carry on in this way without first understanding the fundamental principles of feeding the correct amount of airflow through the rotors. Knowing this will help you recognise the effects of blade sailing and how to avoid it before damage is done to the rotor head, blades and controls.

Having the benefit of a pre-rotator, does however, make gyroplane operation a lot easier, especially if your airstrip is short or is in poor surface condition. Getting airborne in the shortest distance possible does save a  lot of wear and tear on the gyroplane especially if it is without some form of suspension - as most are. It also leaves a greater margin of safety on short strips and those surrounded by obstacles such as tall trees, hedges or phone and electricity cables.

From a professional point of view, being able to control your rotor blades while strapped into your seat does give you and the sport in general more credibility especially when operating as some do - out of Civil or Military airfields. To be able, simply by controlling a lever, to accelerate your rotor blades either whilst taxying or at the holding point, gives a much better impression and is certainly more civilised than having to unbuckle your straps, dismount, pat-up the rotors, re-seat and buckle up again, sometimes more than once before having final take off clearance.

Today, two alternative systems are in popular use - **a gearbox type** and **a flexible shaft type**. A third, **a hydraulic type**, has been seen on some Italian VPM machines but information on them is sparse.

## The Gearbox type

These were originally used around 1970 on some Campbell Crickets and many are still in service today - or have been copied. They are to be found mainly on Volkswagen engines. Operation is by a pivoted throttle lever situated on the left hand side of the seat and connected via a Bowden cable to a pivoted jockey wheel. This in turn, tensioned a small vee belt drive to a small gearbox mounted atop the engine. A later modification replaced the vee belt drive with a friction drum and rubber pulley.

From the gearbox, power is transmitted to the upper unit by a telescopic steel shaft fitted at each end with universal joints. This upper unit comprises a vee belt and pulley reduction drive unit and the small pulley contains a freewheel type bearing that isolates the lower units when rotor blade speed exceeds that of the drive shaft.

*Gearbox type friction drive drum and pulleys on a Volkswagen engine.*

## The Flexible Shaft Type

Known generally as the "Wunderlich Pre-rotator", this type has been developed and marketed by Dick Wunderlich of Illinois, USA. Having evolved over many years, the system is now recognised as the most successful to date, easily adaptable to any of the engine types in current use. The exploded diagram shows all the component parts which can be purchased in kit form from your local gyroplane supplier.

*Gearbox type upper vee pulleys and belt drive showing universal joint at top of telescopic shaft*

The drive drum (41) is mounted to the prop hub. The upper unit (1) to (13) is mounted to the rotor head. When lever (44), conveniently mounted to the seat is pulled, drive wheel (35) contacts the drum. Power is transmitted to the Bendix (8) through the ½" flexible shaft and spur gears. Torque load on the Bendix causes it to spin upwards to engage on the ring gear (2). The

*Wunderlich Pre-rotator - Upper unit showing Bendix drive and ring gear*

Bendix disengages when the lever is released and when the rotor speed exceeds that of the Bendix.

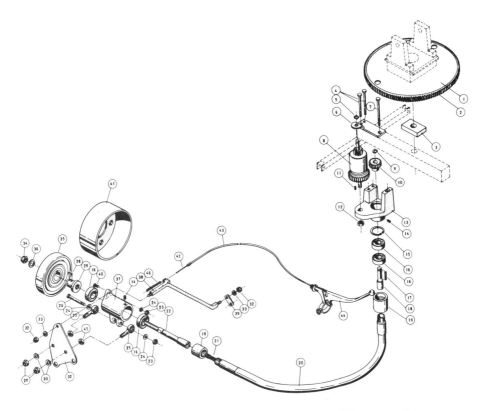

*The Flexible Shaft System - Diagram courtesy of D. Wunderlich*

Operation of a pre-rotator does require a degree of skill and this can only be achieved through experience. If you are lucky enough to own an operator's manual, then this will help to get you started. Only regular use can perfect your skills and hopefully minimise wear and tear on both pre-rotator and gyroplane. It is best to bear in mind that the first 100 rotor r.p.m. is hardest to achieve by manual means and the last 100 r.p.m. is hardest by mechanical means.

*Wunderlich Pre-rotator - Propeller-end unit showing friction wheel and drum*

# Chapter 16

# Wallis Series Gyroplanes

The name of Ken Wallis has been synonymous with autogyros for many years now and this book would not be complete without reference to his many achievements, not only in gyroplane development but also for his efforts in promoting the use of these machines to perform tasks that other types of aerial craft could not do.

Ken Wallis' interest in autogyros started around 1958 while serving with the Strategic Air Command in the United

*Ken Wallis flying his Type WA-116 (XR-943) Autogyro - better known as "Little Nellie" from the James Bond movie "You only Live Twice"*

States. He sent off for a set of plans for a Bensen B-7 Gyroglider but didn't start construction until his return to England. Ken was only interested in a powered machine so the B-7 was modified to take an engine unit and its first flight took place at Shoreham. Due to several shortcomings, this model was scrapped in favour of a completely new machine which Ken designed, taking care to keep the same scale as the B-7 but with much greater stability. This machine, powered by a 76 HP McCulloch engine became the first prototype WA116 and incorporated several unique features which included a flexible shaft pre-rotator and the now widely accepted offset Gimbal Head (which he patented).

When the Army became interested in Ken's autogyro, Beagle Aircraft acquired the contract to build four machines and one of these later became "Little Nellie" of James Bond fame. The Army trials started in 1962 after the WA-116 had undergone a formal flight test and electrical strain gauging programme to "Certificate of Airworthiness" standard. Some 23 service pilots flew the trials autogyros before Army interest turned to helicopters. During the 1980's however, an updated version of the early trials machine, G-ARZC was successfully used in further military trials and exercises both in the UK and Germany. There have also been 25 take-offs and landings on a moving lorry, prior to

flights from very small vessels at sea.

Various experiments with engine alternatives led to a number of later designs, some of which include the WA-117/RR 100 h.p., WA-120/RR 130 h.p., WA-121/Mc 90 h.p., WA-118/M 120 h.p. Meteor, WA-116/L 80 h.p. Limbach and latterly the WA-201/2T twin Rotax 532 experimental machine.

*Ken Wallis with WA-116/F/S G-BLIK, holder of Twelve World Records for Autogyros*

In the mid 1960's, the Wallis WA-116 was operated by the Norfolk and Norwich Aero Club and over 100 pilots had their first gyroplane flights after only a short briefing. The first two seater machine, designed just to give a "feel" of autogyro flight before the first solo, didn't fly until 1969.

Ken Wallis' gyroplanes have held every world record for speed, range, altitude and duration and as well as his promotional work in many films, television programmes and aerial displays, his machines have also been involved in a number of commercial enterprises. These range from police work involving detecting illicit graves, i.e. murder victims using Plessey radar, to scanning Loch Ness in 1970 with a specially silenced Rolls Royce powered WA-117 and infra red sensor equipment in search of the illusive "Nessie". They have also proved their efficiency in the day and night, all-weather post-attack, airfield damage reconnaissance exercise **"Keswick"** in 1987, equipped with infra-red linescan, transmitting imagery to the ground viewing and recording base, in real time.

Ken Wallis' modesty belies his achievements, always insisting that he remains an "enthusiastic amateur". It comes as no surprise to learn that in 1996, he was awarded the MBE for "Services to Autogiros". Ken's knowledge and experience in the field of gyroplane design is invaluable and his opinions on various aspects of safety and engineering principles are still sought by those in authority. Perhaps one day he will be persuaded to market his brand of gyroplane and let us experience the thrill of 007 style flying.

# Chapter 17

# Trailers

For a gyroplane owner, a custom built trailer is almost compulsory equipment. Those lucky enough to be able to store and fly their machines from one location are indeed few and far between - probably in the order of 1 in 10. If you fall outside this category then you must have some means of transporting your gyroplane around, whether it be to and from your local airstrip or workshop or to a rally in some far corner of the country. Most of the trailers I've had the opportunity to see are custom built to suit their owner's individual needs and gyroplane dimensions but whatever style or design you use, always try to make it operable by one person - you! This doesn't imply that you have to be anti-social but there are times when you have to load or unload the trailer almost a million miles from the nearest available help.

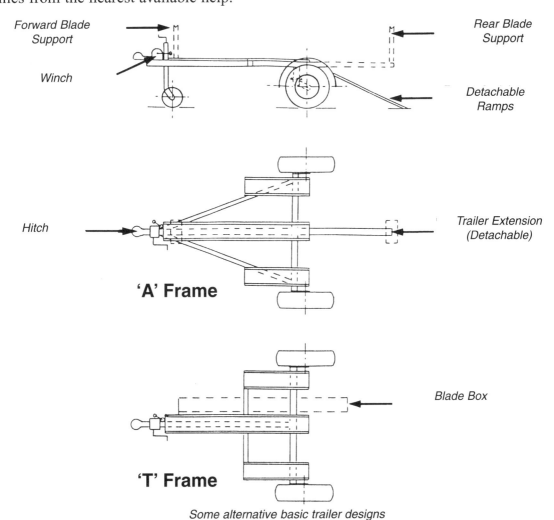

Some alternative basic trailer designs

Most popular type of trailer is either the 'T' or 'A' frame configuration that incorporates basic equipment such as three ramps, hand winch, jockey wheel and good suspension units. Selection of the latter is very important because your gyroplane needs to be protected from all possible road disorders - it is, after all, a flying machine in an unnatural environment and as such, must be transported with great care. Most popular types of suspension are the rubber block "indispension" units and these are available in various load categories depending on the all-up weight being towed. These and most other trailer hardware should be available at your nearest trailer centre or caravan supplier.

Of course, if you want your Gyroplane completely protected from the elements, then you could construct a completely enclosed trailer but this does involve a great deal more time, effort and especially imagination.

One friend I know, has a custom built caravan that not only hangars the gyro, complete with rotors attached but also incorporates living accommodation including bunks, cooker, fridge and the proverbial kitchen sink - now that's luxury. (See above).

**Rotor blades** - how do you transport them? Two schools of thought apply here so its up to you to decide the best alternative to suit your particular circumstances.

a) It has been said that to avoid possible damage to the rotor head system, it is better to

remove the rotor blades from the gyroplane and transport them separately in a custom built box. This involves removing the whole assembly at the teeter bolt and, when down at a handleable level, disconnect one of the blades at the hub bar blocks. Both can then be transferred to the blade box and attached securely either to the trailer or roof rack of your car.

*Typical lightweight trailer combination transported with blades intact*

The disadvantages of this method are threefold.

1.    Whenever you want to fly the machine, the blades have to be re-rigged and set up at a very precise angle (usually 2° positive) and then hoisted atop the gyroplane to locate on the teeter bolt. This is usually a 2-person operation although, with a struggle it is possible to do on your own.

2.    The hub bar/blade attachment bolts and the teeter bolt are regularly being subjected to wear, tear and unnecessary stressing.

3.    When you've finished your days flying, the whole process has to be repeated, but in reverse order.

b) The alternative method is to transport your gyroplane with rotor blades left intact, securely held in the fore and aft position. Obviously, both blades have to be supported but this can be done quite easily. The front blade will need a vertical support about three quarters of its length out from the teeter bolt - this usually ends up near to the winch and can be secured either with bolts through the trailer chassis or by a specially made attachment bracket welded in position.

The rear blade support is accommodated with a simple detachable rearward extension of the trailer using the same method of attachment as the front support.

*Another variation of an enclosed trailer*

Care should be taken to ensure both blades rest in-line or, better still, slightly higher than the hub bar and that the contact surfaces are protected to avoid chaffing damage. It's a good idea to have a set of blade covers made - they will protect your expensive blades not only from the elements but also from nicks and scratches caused by stone chips and other debris thrown up from the road.

By way of experience, I've used method b) since 1982 without any sign of damage to my rotor head system and I find it a much easier and more convenient way of transportation.

The legal requirements and law of trailers including overall maximum dimensions and lighting regulations are covered in the current edition of Motor Vehicle Construction and Use regulations. This is available from H.M. Stationery Offices or from the Motoring Organisations or the Police.

Whatever style of trailer you design, always make sure it has a sturdy means of securing your gyro. All three wheels should be securely held in position without the possibility of shaking loose through buffeting and if the rotor blades remain intact, secure them to the supports with clamps or bungees.

If possible, make provision on the trailer for storing and securing the ramps and don't forget to always carry a spare wheel and jack. Aim for a trailer noseweight of about 50lbs (23 kg) - this seems to be about right for the all-up weight being towed and should be quite stable.

Rear lighting is usually accommodated with a standard "trailer board" unit mounted as far to the rear as is possible. These units comprise all the basic legal lighting arrangements with space for your number plate and a suitable length of 7-core cable included. This method seems by far the best, considering what's involved in designing your own system and purchasing your own parts.

On a cautionary note - don't hurry the process of loading the trailer - the security of your gyroplane is paramount. It can be so easy to miss that tie or clamp especially if you get distracted away from your task. Try to be single minded about it and then check and re-check that everything's been secured. Make a little clamp to stop the rudder flapping around - this can be secured in the slot between fin and rudder. Finally, the most rearward part of your load should carry a brightly coloured piece of material in order to warn those following you where the "tail" of your cargo is.

## Chapter 18

# Air Command Series Gyroplanes

The Air Command Series of Gyroplanes originated in the United States, and the first examples appeared on the British Register early in 1988. In the USA they were classed as Ultralights (the same as British Microlights) provided they were powered only by the Rotax 477 engine, but in the UK they came under the normal Gyroplane definition and were all equipped from new with either the Rotax 503 air-cooled engine, or the more powerful 532 liquid-cooled engine.

*The original Air Command single seater with Rotax 532cc engine*

It is quite a sophisticated Gyroplane, and boasts a quiet engine/prop combination undercarriage suspension, rotor pre-spin, rotor brake, composite rotors, and main-wheel disc brakes all as standard equipment, with long range tanks and a pilot nacelle a optional extras. At a later stage, the Rotax 582 engine became a further option.

The gyroplanes were imported by Skyrider Aviation of Coventry who sold them eithe as kits, or as completed aircraft. As a result of this latter function, the operation wa deemed to be a commercial venture, and the aircraft were initially handled exclusivel by the CAA, with the PFA only becoming involved at a later stage when a substantia number of aircraft had been sold for individuals to complete themselves. In all, some 6 aircraft were sold in the UK

A two-seater was available for training purposes, but a number of people continued t do their training on their own aircraft, down the already approved single-seater route.

Between April 1989 and March 1991, there were a number of fatal accidents to th 532 powered aircraft, and whilst these were never attributed to any one single cause, i March 1991 the CAA issued a Temporary Suspension order on **all** Air Comman **Permits-to-Fly.**

After a thorough investigation by the A.A.I.B. and exhaustive flight testing b approved test pilots, a series of recommended modifications were finally agreed by th

*The latest Air Command single seater with Upgrade kit*

CAA. These modifications involved quite a few fundamental changes to the machine and all had to be complied with and inspected before a permit was renewed.

Several machines had already been cleared for flight, when in 1996 another fatality occurred - this time to a modified machine. Frustratingly, the **A.A.I.B.** were unable to draw a satisfactory conclusion as to the cause and in February 1999, the **CAA** decided not to issue **permits to fly** on any Air Command types. More recently however, there are moves afoot to re-introduce a drastically modified Air Command, and I do mean drastically.

The **British Rotorcraft Association's** current Engineering Officer Gerry Speich, has taken on the task, with the co-operation of the **CAA**, of bringing the aircraft into line with recent technological research carried out by the **University of Glasgow**. The major modification involves a re-design that brings the centre-line of thrust much closer to the machine's centre of gravity. An upgrade kit which also includes a horizontal stabiliser should, if successful, enable existing UK Air Command owners to relatively quickly and simply, update their aircraft to this new standard. At the time of printing, the re-certification programme progresses well, but results will obviously take time.

# Chapter 19

# Airworthiness and Flight Safety

## by Robin F. Morton

## Airworthiness

As is mentioned elsewhere in this book, new Gyroplane designs must now comply with BCAR Section "T", and all machines must be maintained in accordance with the Owners Manual, which is published by the PFA, and administered by the Inspection network.

Nevertheless, for all Gyroplanes, a long-standing Airworthiness problem exists which stems from the misguided impression that because Gyroplane construction looks extremely simple (which is true), therefore everything connected with them can somehow be skimped or be a bit slapdash. **Nothing** could be further from the truth! It is still an **aircraft,** and must be treated as such, or it will bite you. Think of it this way - if you use a set of sub-standard bolts or other parts in its construction because it's cheaper or easier and no-one will know, how will you feel about it when you are at 1000ft and looking down on a very small world, because rest assured, **you** will know. The same comment applies to the plethora of (frequently) unauthorised and unapproved modifications which appear on Gyroplanes - it is not difficult to have them approved, provided the idea is basically sound, you supply some drawings or photographs to the PFA, and discuss the whole thing with your Inspector before you start.

As well as the PFA Approved maintenance which must be carried out on a Gyroplane over a period of time to ensure it remains airworthy, there are various other items which need to be in place to make the aircraft legal before it is flown:

1.     The aircraft must be registered with the CAA in your name.

2.     You must be in possession of a valid Permit-to-Fly for the aircraft, and a Flight Release Certificate, signed by your Inspector on an annual basis.

3.     A brand new aircraft must be test-flown for the first time by an experienced and properly licensed  Gyroplane Pilot.

Nothing in all the above is either difficult or insurmountable, and both the PFA and the BRA are dedicated to helping you to achieve **safe** and **enjoyable** flying with your Gyro. Talk to them, or to any of the Gyroplane Inspectors, and they will give you all the help and advice you need.

## Flight Safety

This is a cautionary tale, and I urge all potential Gyronauts to read on!

As you have seen in other parts of this book, Gyroplanes have been around for a very long time, and were first conceived by Juan de la Cierva to overcome the inherent stall/spin accidents prevalent in fixed-wing aircraft of the era. Even so, Gyroplanes still obey the basic laws of aerodynamics, and need to be operated within their own, very special, flight envelope, which largely involves avoiding negative or zero 'g' manoeuvres.

It is totally irrelevant how many hours you already have in your Log Book, flying any other sort of aeroplane, be it fixed-wing, flex-wing, or helicopter,

## A GYROPLANE IS COMPLETELY DIFFERENT!!

No amount of experience in other aircraft will prepare you for it, and without adequate Gyroplane instruction, even 'low hops' can be dangerous, or at the very best, expensive. It is a sad fact that at least two fatal Gyroplane accidents in the U.K. were caused by the owners flying them without instruction, and they both occurred soon after take-off, and therefore from no great height. A part of the problem may be that the original American building instructions for Bensen aircraft included a section on self-taught flying, but events have shown that doing it that way can be *extremely dangerous*. It is also **illegal** to do it in the UK. It may seem the most obvious thing to say, but -

## DO NOT FLY WITHOUT INSTRUCTION

I am sure you would not consider climbing into a fixed-wing aircraft and trying to fly it without any tuition or prior knowledge of what you were doing, but too many people still think that it is all right to do so in a Gyroplane.

A Gyroplane tends to live in your garage, rather than at an airfield, and you can tow it to any strip of level ground and fly it (provided you have the permission of the landowner, and he doesn't live beside Heathrow), and that freedom is one of its star advantages. The downside is that if you do that by yourself in the early stages without first receiving any instruction, "just to taxy about a bit", a combination of enthusiasm and natural exuberance may well get the better of you, and before you know it, you are inadvertently airborne, out of control, frightened silly, and about to become a statistic. Even unsupervised taxying can cause damage to the rotor head which may not manifest itself until you are flying.

Remember, a Gyroplane is an aircraft, not a toy, so treat it with the respect it demands and deserves. Do yourself, your family, and the movement the greatest favour you can -
**FLY CAREFULLY**

Happy landings!

# Chapter 20

# P.F.A. Gyroplane Inspectors & Flying Instructors

## Inspectors

**Mr David Beevers** (Inspector No 722) Pocklington, Yorkshire.　　Tel: 01759-303315

**Mr Carl Butler** (008) Coventry, Warwickshire.　　Tel: 01203-402975

**Mr David Charity** (687) Towcester, Northants.　　Tel: 01127-811569

**Mr Woody de Saar** (715) Great Yarmouth, Norfolk.　　Tel: 01493-332794
or 0771-2239693

**Mr Kieran Donaghy** (686) Middlesex　　Tel: 01705-640182

**Mr Richard Everett** (682) Ipswich, Suffolk.　　Tel: 01473-747685

**Mr John Ferguson** (680) Ayrshire.　　Tel: 01465-714827

**Mr Rob Fidler** (702) Northern Ireland.　　Tel: 00353-743-1583 or 07802-210216

**Mr Andrew Grieve** (357) Aberdeenshire.　　Tel: 01464-444240

**Mr Mark Hayward** (683) Cornwall.　　Tel: 01752-272360 or (evenings) 01503-240822

**Mr Bert Jarvis** (296) Fife.　　Tel: 01337-830042 or 0410-464058

**Mr Stewart Jones** (681) Dyfed.　　Tel: 01974-298075

**Mr Tony Melody** (679) Hillingdon, Middlesex.　　Tel: 0208-573-6918 or 0956-447085

**Mr Robin Morton** (311) Cheltenham, Gloucestershire.　　Tel: 01285-720980

**Mr Roger Savage** (685) Penrith, Cumbria.　　Tel: 01768-483859 or 07836-272033

**Mr Ernie Simmons** (196) Boston, Lincs.　　Tel: 01205-362815 (day)

**Mr Gordon Smith** (491) Dunkeswell, Devon.　　Tel: 01404-891506

**Mr Gerry Speich** (707) Warwickshire.　　Tel: 01926-484559

**Mr Tom Stoddart** (336) Carlisle, Cumbria.　　Tel: 01228-573001 or 01228-41601

**Mr John Torring** (442) Bournemouth, Dorset.　　Tel: 01202-511282 or 07802-759280

# Flying Instructors

E  **Mr David Beevers,** Yapham Mill, Pocklington, York YO4 2PB

Flight training on various types. Fees tba.　　　　　　Tel: 01759-303315

**Mr Woody de Saar,** Bond Helicopters, North Denes Airfield, Great Yarmouth
NR30 5TF
Training on Parsons 2 place, or own gyro.　　　　　　Tel: 01493-332794
　　　　　　　　　　　　　　　　　　　　　　　　　　　or 0771-2239693

**Mr Mike Goldring,** 6 Coombeshead Rd, Highweek, Newton Abbot, Devon
 TQ12 1PY

Flight training on RAF 2000.　　　　　　　　　　　　Tel: 01626-353717

**Mr Patrick Howell,** 6 Millers Bank, Broom, Alcester, Warwickshire B50 4HZ
　　　　　　　　　　　　　　　　　　　　　　Tel/Fax: 01789-773801

**Mr Marc Lhermette,** The Old Farmhouse, Lamberhurst Farm, Dargate, Faversham,
Kent ME13 9EP

Flight training from Lydd and Manston.　　　　　　　Tel: 01227-750328

E  **Mr Tony Melody,** 103 Polehill Rd, Hillingdon, Middlesex UB10 0QD.

Flight training on RAF 2000. Fees by arrangement. Reduced rates for groups of 2-3.
Training at Henstridge Airfield, Somerset.　　　　　　Tel: 0208-5736918
　　　　　　　　　　　　　　　　　　　　　　　　　　　or 07956-447085

E  **Mr Roger Savage,** Croft House, Berrier, Greystoke, Penrith, Cumbria CA11 0XD.

Training from Carlisle and other locations on RAF 2000, VPM M16, Montgomeries,
Crickets, Bensens etc. Fees tba.　　　　　　　　　　Tel: 01768-483859
　　　　　　　　　　　　　　　　　　　　　　　　　　　or 07836-272033
　　　　　　　　　　　　　E-mail: gyroplanes@rogersavage.co.uk

E  **Mr Tony Unwin,** 'Harts', Stone Allerton, Somerset BS26 2NW.

Training from Henstridge, Pembrey, Bristol and Swansea on VPM M16 and Crickets.
Fees tba.

　　　　　　　　　　　　　　　　　　　　　　　Tel: 01934-712110.
　　　　　　　　　　　　　　　　　　　　　　E-mail: gyfly@aol.com

E - also examiners.

**Chapter 21**

# Contact Addresses

## Manufacturers, agents and importers

**Montgomerie Autogyros,** Kirkmichael Road, Crosshill, Maybole, Ayrshire, Scotland, KA19 7RJ                                                                 Tel. 01655-740339

**Newtonair Gyroplanes Ltd.,** 6 Coombeshead Road, Highweek, Newton Abbott, Devon, TQ12 1PY                                                                 Tel. 01626-353717

**Everett Autogyros,** Abbey Oakes, Sproughton, Ipswich, Suffolk IP8 3DD
Tel. 01473-747685
Fax. 01473-748951

**Dragon Wings Rotors,** Rotor Flight Dynamics (UK) Ltd., 29 Templegate Close, Whitkirk, Leeds, Yorkshire, LS 15 0PJ.                     Tel./Fax.0113-2644945

**Layzell Gyroplanes Ltd.,** 17 Courtfield Road, Quedgeley, Gloucester, GL2 4UQ.
Tel./Fax. 01452-723541

## Principal Engine Suppliers and Remanufacturers

**Skydrive Ltd.,** (Rotax), "Burnside", Deppers Bridge, Southam, Warwickshire.
Tel. 01926-612188
Fax.01926-613781

**Acro Engines Ltd.,** (Volkswagen parts and aero instruments), Turners Arms Farm, Yearby, Redcar, TS11 8HH.                                             Tel. 01642-470322

**Volkspares,** 104 Newlands Park, Sydenham, London, SE26 5NA    Tel. 0208-7787766
Fax. 0208-6769619

**German and Swedish Car Centre Ltd.,** (Volkswagen), Space Way, North Feltham Trading Estate, Feltham, Middlesex, TW14 OTH                      Tel. 0208-8931688

## Associations, Aviation suppliers and other useful Addresses

**British Rotorcraft Association,** (Memberships), Peter Cresswell, "Five Farthings", The Green, Great Bourton, Banbury, Oxon, OX17 IQH          Tel/Fax. 01295-750773

**Popular Flying Association,** Terminal Building, Shoreham Airport, Shoreham-by-Sea, West Sussex BN4 5FF.                                  Tel. 01273-461616

**CAA Central Library-Aircraft Registrations,** CAA House, 45-59 Kingsway, London, WC2B 6TE.

**CAA Flight Crew Licencing,** Civil Aviation Authority, Aviation House, South Area, Gatwick Airport, Sussex, RH6 0YR

**Civil Aviation Authority,** (Printing and Publications), Contact:- Documedia Ltd.,37 Windsor Street, Cheltenham, Glos, GL52 2DG.                 Tel. 01242-235151

**B.M.A.A.,** The Bullring, Deddington, Oxford, OX5 4TT            Tel. 01869-38888

**The Aviation Bookshop,** 656 Holloway Road, London, N19 3PD

**Transair Pilot Shop - Transair (UK) Ltd.,** Shoreham Airport, Shoreham-By-Sea, West Sussex BN43 5PA.                                  Tel: 01273-466007
                                                                   Fax: 01273-462246

**Pilot Warehouse,** The Old Hospital, Aldbury, Tring, Herts. HP23 5SF
                                                                   Tel: 01442-851087
                                                                   Fax: 01442-851541

**R.D. Aviation,** 25 Bankside, Kidlington, Oxon. OX5 1JE.          Tel: 01865-841441
                                                                   Fax: 01865-842495

**Light Aero Spares Ltd.,** Shebbear, Beaworthy, Devon EX21 5RQ.  Tel: 01409-281578
                                                                   Fax: 01409-281680

**Microlight Sport Aviation Ltd.,** Chatteris Airfield, Cambridge. Tel/Fax: 020-8325-0197

**Skycraft Ltd.,** Kestrel, Broadgate, Weston Hills, Spalding PE12 6DP Tel: 0870-7592723
                                                                   Fax: 08700-7592723

**Harry Mendelssohn Discount Sales,** 49-51 Colington Road, Edinburgh EH10 5DH.
                                                                   Tel: 0131-447-7777
                                                                   Fax: 0131-452-9004

**Comunica Helmets & Headsets,** Comunica Industries International Ltd., St Catherine's Mead, Kingsgate Road, Winchester SO23 9QQ.           Tel: 01962-840084
                                                                   Fax: 01962-856685

**Dick Wunderlich (pre-rotators),** 306W 16th St., Lockport, Illinois 60441, USA
Tel: (815) 838-0450

**Reconditioned ICOM Batteries - Lloyd-Hughes,** 29 Godre Mynydd, Gwernymynydd, Mold, Flintshire CH7 4AD.
Tel: 01352-757403
E-mail: huw@iron99.freeserve.co.uk

**USA - Popular Rotorcraft Association,** Contact at their website: www.pra.org.
Tel/Fax: (219)353-7227
E-mail: prahq@aol.com

**France - FFPLUM - Federation Francais de Planeur Ultra-leger Motorise.**
Website: www.interpc.fr/ffplum/

**Australia - ASRA - The Australian Sport Rotorcraft Association inc.**
Website: www.asra.org.au/

**New Zealand - The New Zealand Autogyro Association.** Website: www.raanz.org.nz/

**Ireland - SARC - Society of Amateur Rotorcraft Constructors (all Ireland).** Contact: Johnston Fitzgerald
Tel: 028427-72611
E-mail: jjfitzgyro@aol.com

**South Africa - South African Gyrocopter Pilots Association.** Contact: Eric Torr
Tel: (011)391-6426
E-mail: gyrosa@netactive.co.za

# Magazines

**Fly Gyro** Magazine, Edited and Published by Mel. N. Morris-Jones, Barle Crest, Lady Street, Dulverton, TA22 9DB
Tel. 01398-323903
E-mail: mel@flygiro.com

**Rotor Gazette International,** Edited by Roland Parsons, Llangeitho Times Publishing, Tregaron, Dyfed, SY25 6QU
Tel. 01974-821205
Website: www.llangeitho.co.uk

**International Autogyro 1/41y,** Edited and Published by Ron Bartlett, 9 Layton Road, Parkstone, Poole, Dorset, BH12 2BH
Tel: 01202-741581

# Books

**"Short Hops"** by Shirley Jennings (Gyroplane Aviatrix) in A4 Softback.

This privately published book is a comprehensive narrative of Shirley's personal experiences from her first trip in a Gyro-Glider, through the Gyroplane building process and onto the completion of her P.P.L.(G) and more. Written in an "easy to read" style, the subjects covered include understanding the basic Gyroplane and its various components, rotor flight theory and some 'in flight' experiences not to be missed. Shirley's understanding of both the Gyroplane and its flight characteristics will provide an early learning tool for ab-initio students and enthusiasts alike and her bubbling enthusiasm for this type of flying comes roaring out at you from its pages. A highly recommended book that is available direct from: **Ms Shirley Jennings, 4 Parc-an-Drea, Whitecross Road, Cury, Helston, Cornwall, TR12 7BJ. Price: £15.00 including p&p.**

**"Gyroplanes - A Guide to their Construction and Operation"** by Hugh Bancroft-Wilson in softback.

This is the new 2001 LTP updated fifth edition of this excellent Gyro. book. It details everything you need to know about building and maintaining a Gyroplane, from drilling holes in aircraft grade aluminium to getting your licence - even trailers are covered in this very comprehensive edition. Plastic comb bound in wipe clean covers so you can keep it to hand in the workshop. 103 pages with many diagrams plus colour plates. Available direct from: **Llangeitho Times Publishing, Tregaron, Dyfed, SY25 6QU.**
**Price: £13.95 inc. UK p&p., Europe p&p £2.50, World p&p £3.50.**
Tel. 01974-821205

**"Owners Handbook for Ultralight Gyroplanes"** by Peter Lovegrove. An essential technical book for all Gyroplane owners and operators - available from: The Popular Flying Association's office at Shoreham. POA.

**"Syllabus for the Private Pilot's Licence Course (2 seat Gyroplane)"** by Mac Smith.

**"Syllabus for the Assistant Flying Instructor's Course (2 seat Gyroplane)"** by Mac Smith.

**"Technical Questions for Gyroplane student pilots",** by David Charity.

All these are available from: Peter Cresswell, "Five Farthings", 7 The Green, Great Bourton, Banbury, Oxon, OX17 1QH. **Priced each at £9.00. + £1.50 p&p.**
Tel./Fax. 01295-750773.

**CAA CAP 53 (Flight Crew Licencing),** Documedia, 37 Windsor Street, Cheltenham, Glos, GL52 2DG.
Tel. 01242-235151

**"Pooley's Flight Guide".** Available from: Pooleys Flight Guides Ltd, Elstree Aerodrome, Herts, WD6 3AW
Tel. 0208-207-3749
Fax: 0208-953-2512

# Videos

**"RGI Wallis Days 1997"** The first ever Wallis Days, held at Shipdham Airfield, Norfolk and a unique record of this special event. **£11.75 + £2.50 p&p**

**"Weston Super Gyro Day"** The 1996 Helidays event, held each year on the seafront at Weston-super-Mare but this time featuring lots of Gyroplanes. Plenty to see including lots of flying shots. **£11.75 + £2.50p&p.**

**"My World of Gyroplanes"** This latest video contains plenty of everything including Wallis Days 1999, the White Horses Flight 1999 plus many other short clips including that of the late Chris Julian in action. **£14.25 + £2.50 p&p.**

**All these are available from: Dave Organ, Apex Productions, Marshall House, Wymans Lane. Cheltenham. Glos. GL 51 9QF.** **Tel: 01242-233084**
**Fax: 01242-690034**

# Aviation Insurance

**Hayward Aviation Ltd.,** Harling House, 47 - 51 Great Suffolk Street, London, SEl OBS.
Tel. 0207-9027800
Fax. 0207-9288041

**Traffords Aviation Insurance,** Traffords Ltd., Franklin House, Steppingly Road, Flitwick, Bedford, MK45 lAJ
Tel. 0870-9000-331
Fax. 0870-9000-332

**H.R Jennings & Co. Ltd.,** Aviation House, 61 Brighton Road, South Croydon, Surrey, XR2 6ED
Tel. 020-8680-0688
Fax. 020-8688-5109

**Independent Underwriting Services Ltd.,** Dodle House, Oldham Road, Denshaw, Oldham, Lancs. OL3 5RP
Tel. 01457-877458
Fax. 01457-871213

**Bartlett Insurance Brokers,** Broadway Hall, Horsforth, Leeds, LS18 4RS
Tel. 0113-2585711
Fax. 0113-2585081

# Chapter 22

# Gyroplane Glossary

**Advancing Blade -** The portion of the rotor disc in which the rotation of the blade is moving in the direction of the aircraft's travel.

**Aerodynamics -** Hydrodynamics and aerodynamics are both branches of fluid dynamics, which is the study of fluids in motion. The fundamental laws governing the movements of gases such as air, and liquids such as water, are identical. Although many liquids are almost incompressible.

The equations representing these **natural laws** are, however, so complex that although formulated over a hundred years ago, they cannot be easily solved to account for all situations and conditions. The equations which describe in a general fashion the motion of fluids were developed in 1820 and subsequently perfected by G.G. Stokes.

At the beginning of the present century, aerodynamics was introduced with the possibility of flight in air. It started with the same assumption as hydrodynamics with the added assumption of incompressibility replacing what was a fact for water.

**Aerofoil -** A surface designed to produce lift from the movement of air over it. Ideally, it should present the greatest amount of lift with the least amount of drag.

**Anodizing -** Anodizing is the deposition of a thin film of synthetic oxide on a light metal, such as aluminium, to prevent the further access of air to the surface, preserving the lustre and preventing corrosion. The article is made to anode in 3% solution of chromic acid at about 104 degreesF. The voltage is gradually increased to a maximum of 50 volts and the process may take an hour. Sulphuric and oxalic acid processed are also used, and the anodic film may be dyed various colours.

**Autogyro -** A heavier-than-air flying machine which derives its lift from a rotor system mounted above the machine, with blades rotating more or less horizontally.

**Autorotation -** A flight condition made possible by the vertical or horizontal movement of air through the rotor system.

**Blade Loading -** The load placed on the rotor blades of a gyroplane, determined by dividing the gross weight of the craft by the total combined areas of all blades (not the disc area, but the blade area).

**Balance -** Rotor blades that are equal in weight will balance each other. Unbalanced rotor blades may cause control stick shake and instability when in flight.

**Bank -** Sideward tilt of the aircraft in flight. When correctly executed, the bank compensates for centrifugal force, and the passengers will be pressed straight down in their seats.

**Ceiling -** The maximum altitude to which a gyroplane can climb. Because of thin air, the engine decreases in power, or the rotor blades no longer provide lift to climb.

**Centre of Gravity -** Called C of G. A point where the resultant of all weight forces will hang evenly from this point. Usually at, or very near to the main mast.

**Centre of Pressure -** An imaginary point on the cord lines of all the rotor blades where all the aerodynamic forces of the aerofoil surfaces are concentrated.

**Centrifugal Force -** The force caused by the rotation of an object with mass.

**Chord -** A straight line between the exact centre of the leading and trailing edge of the rotor blade.

**Chordwise Balance -** A term that refers to the mass balance of an aerofoil. It is designed to be in the centre of lift.

**Compressibility -** Forces acting on a rotor blade when its tip speed approaches the speed of sound.

**Coning -** The blades tend to bend upwards in flight, when they are lifting the aircraft. Referred to as the coning angle.

**Cruise Speed -** An airspeed that usually results in the best fuel economy and is usually between ½ and ⅔ of full power.

**Density Altitude -** Pressure altitude calculated from air temperature, altitude and humidity.

**Disc -** The area swept by the blades of the rotor.

**Disc Loading -** The gross weight of the gyroplane divided by the rotor disc area. The greater the disc loading, the gyroplane's sinking speed will increase, and its glide-angle will become steeper.

**Dissymmetry of Lift -** The unequal lift across the rotor disc, caused from the advancing blade creating more lift than the retreating blade.

**Dynamic Roll Over -** A roll over on the ground caused by violent rotor flapping. Caused by insufficient rotor rpm combined with excessive ground speed.

**Downwind -** Flying with the wind direction. Flying downwind near the ground is dangerous, true airspeed is lower than groundspeed and the aircraft's lift is less.

**Endurance -** The maximum length of time a gyroplane can stay aloft on its fuel supply.

**Flapping -** The up and down motion of the rotor blade on its hinge. Without flapping a gyroplane would roll over on its side during flight because of the unequal lift of the rotor disc.

**Flare -** A landing manoeuvre performed near the ground to slow the gyroplane's rate of descent and air speed. The gyroplane is in a nose-high attitude during the execution of this manoeuvre.

**Flutter -** A self-induced oscillating motion of improperly designed rotor blades.

**Ground Effect - (also known as ground cushion) -** A beneficial increase in lift near the ground. Readily apparent when the rotor height is one-half of the rotor's diameter over the ground. Less engine power is required due to the air being thrust downward to meet the ground. This denser air is partially trapped beneath the rotor disc.

**Ground Vortex -** The horizontal whirlwind that forms at the forward edge of the rotor wake when the gyroplane flies at low speeds close to the ground.

**Gyroplane -** An aircraft whose lift is developed by the rotor blade system using the principles of autorotation.

**Horsepower Loading -** The ratio of gross weight to horsepower, obtained by dividing the total weight by the engine's horsepower rating.

**Induced Power -** The power associated with developing rotor thrust from the movement of air passing the rotor blade.

**Induced Velocity -** The downward air velocity generated in the process of developing rotor thrust.

**Laminar Flow and Turbulent Flow -** The air flow immediately against the rotor blade (boundary layer) is of most importance in the efficiency of the blade.

Two kinds of fluid flow are possible - **laminar and turbulent.** In laminar flow, the fluid moves as a series of **sheets** or **laminae,** sliding one over the next where there is a difference of speed between them (velocity gradient).

In turbulent flow, particles of fluid (air) can move in any direction - only the mean velocity and direction being defined. This flow can be caused by the overall shape of the object (rotor blade) or disturbances in the surface polish have a noticeable effect on efficiency.

**Laminar Flow Blades -** Laminar Flow Blades are fibreglass blades which cause unusually low drag in the rotorcraft operation. During World War II when experimental planes began to approach the speed of sound, laminar-flow wing sections contributed to its success. In the beginning development stages, thin gauges of sheet metal were used in forming the "skin". It was determined that the slightest buckle forming in the "skin", caused by a counter-sunk rivet, could nullify the advantages of the blade section. With the advent of fibreglass, it was determined that the blade could carry as much load as aluminium-alloy sheets, but had a much greater resistance to damage and guaranteed a smoother surface. Continuing development of these materials has resulted in stronger bonding methods and resins which in turn have led to the laminar-flow rotor system currently being offered for rotorcraft.

**Lead-Lag -** The tip movement needed to adjust the rotor blades in a two-bladed system to get the weight of the whole rotor exactly equal on each side of the main shaft laterally.

**Life -** The recommended safe duration (in hours or measurable wear on the component) of any part on an aircraft. This length of time is determined by either fatigue failure or the operational wear on the part.

**Load Factor -** The ratio of rotor thrust to gross weight of the gyroplane.

**Mast -** The main structural member of the gyroplane. The mast is the vertical assembly that connects the rotor blades to the airframe.

**Parasite Power -** The power used to overcome the drag of all nonlifting components of the rotorcraft.

**Pattern -** The in-plane alignment of all rotor blades so they perfectly balance each other.

**Period -** The time it takes for an oscillating system to complete one full cycle.

**P.I.O. - Pilot Induced Oscillation -** Caused by delays in the human reaction time. Also known as porpoising, which is caused by over control and inexperience.

**Pitch -** The angle between a blade's chord line and a plane perpendicular to the rotor bearing.

**Power Loading -** The ratio of the gross weight to the horsepower rating of the rotorcraft's engine.

**Pull Out -** A flight manoeuvre at the bottom of a dive or descent.

**Push Over -** A flight manoeuvre at the top of a climb or a nose-down dive from level flight.

**Radius of Action -** The maximum distance a gyroplane can fly down and return to without refueling.

**Range -** The maximum distance a gyroplane can fly without landing or refueling.

**Redundancy -** A fail-safe design which provides a secondary standby structural member.

**Retreating Blade -** This blade is on the opposite side of the advancing blade. It travels with the wind created by the forward motion of the rotorcraft.

**Roll -** Tilt of the gyroplane along its longitudinal axis. Controlled by lateral movements of the joystick.

**Rotor -** The lift-producing aerofoil system of a rotorcraft. Rotor blade refers to a single blade only.

**Service Ceiling -** The altitude at which the rotorcraft still maintains the potential to climb at 100 feet per minute.

**Side Force** - The force on the side of a rotor craft due to a side slip.

**Slip** - The controlled flight of a rotorcraft in a direction not in line with its fore and aft axis.

**Solidity Ratio** - The portion of the rotor disc which is filled by the rotor blades. A ratio of the total blade area to the total disc area.

**Spar** - The main load-carrying member of the rotor blade's structure. It carries the centrifugal force as well as loads from the root attachments to the tip of the blade.

**Speed Stability** - The tendency of the rotor craft to pitch up or down when the forward speed is changed.

**Stall** - The separation of the airflow from the surface of the aerofoil or any other component. The resulting loss of lift is a stall.

**Static Stability** - The tendency of a rotorcraft to return to its original flight condition after a disturbance.

**Teetering Rotor** - A two-bladed rotor with a single horizontal hinge for flapping.

**Thickness Ratio** - The ratio of maximum thickness of the aerofoil to the chord length of the aerofoil.

**Thrust** - The rotor force perpendicular to the tip path plane.

**Tip Path Plane** - The plane in which the tip paths travel when the blades are rotating.

**Tip Speed** - The airspeed at the tip of the rotor blade in flight.

**Tip Stall** - The stall condition of the retreating blade which occurs at high forward speeds (approx. 150mph).

**Torque** - A rotary force. A reaction to the turning effort supplied by the engine is an example.

**Tracking** - Rigging the rotor so that each blade passes through the same slot of air.

**Ultralight Gyroplane** - A single engined gyroplane whose maximum all up take-off weight does not exceed **600kg** as defined in the British Civil Airworthiness Requirements (BCAR) Section T. The term **"Ultralight"** has become a generic term that covers any 2 seat light aircraft less than 900kg AUW, and is considered to be the UK version of the American "Microlight".

**Yaw** - Turning of the gyroplane to the right or left by changing the direction of the airflow over the tail surface through the use of the foot pedals.

# About the Author

**Dave Organ** is a Gloucestershire lad whose interest in flying, like most lads of his era, started with building Kiel Kraft model aircraft kits. He took his first flight in a real aeroplane, an Avro Anson, while a member of the schools' Air Training Corps. but on leaving school, decided not to pursue an aviation career. Instead, he trained and qualified as a mechanical engineer and after several years working in industry, gave it up for the motor trade. His interest in flying was rekindled by an old friend from his Karting days who had recently gained his PPL(A) and offered to take him up for a local flight.

Bitten by the bug, Dave then gained his PPL(A) in the minimum 40 hours and went on to enjoy many hours flying the local club Cessna's. It wasn't to last, however and a chance encounter at a motor racing event at Brands Hatch in Kent and again at a flying display at Old Warden in Bedfordshire with "Little Nellie" and Wing Commander Ken Wallis, convinced Dave that there really was **flying after flying**.

It wasn't easy in those days however to find information on this form of flying and after a frustrating search of bookshelves, making telephone calls and letter writing to numerous organisations around the world, he was directed to an address only 15 miles away from home. There, a certain Mr R. Morton had just completed the restoration of a Campbell Cricket gyroplane and wanted to sell it. He did. That was in 1981 and **G - AXVM** is still owned and regularly flown by Dave around the country today.

In 1985, Dave became the co-ordinator of the **Southern Gyroplane Strut** of the PFA and consequently dealt with many worldwide inquiries about the sport. Continually directing these enquiries along the same route, he came to realise that some form of printed matter was needed, not only to minimise the paper workload and time involved but also to make the search for information on Gyroplanes much easier to find; hence the birth of **"A Guide to Gyroplanes in Britain"**.

As one of the original founders of the **British Rotorcraft Association**, Dave still devotes much of his time to Gyroplane matters and although very busy with his own business, can usually be seen and contacted at most of the Gyroplane events held up and down the country.